THE COMPLETE MEDITERRANEAN DIET COOKBOOK

QUICK AND EASY RECIPES FOR A DELICIOUS AND HEALTHY MEDITERRANEAN DIET WITH 30-DAY MEAL PLAN AND A SHOPPING LIST

D1736588

SERENA FOSTER

TABLE OF CONTENTS

INTRODUCTION

Story of the Mediterranean Diet

The Mediterranean diet is a dietary regime, typical of countries in the Mediterranean area, that many studies have linked to countless health benefits, especially in the prevention of cancer, cardiovascular and neurodegenerative diseases, and in 2010 it has been declared by UNESCO an Intangible Heritage of Humanity.. It is a lifestyle that is more than a simple way of eating, more of an eating pattern but, rather, a set of knowledge, social practices, and cultural traditions that have been historically passed down by people living in the Mediterranean. since the post-war period.

How was the Mediterranean Diet born?

The first observational study that led to the explanation of the concept of the "Mediterranean diet" and to understand its benefits, which became popular as the "study of seven countries", was conducted by American biologist and physiologist Ancel Keys in the 1940s.

He moved to the village of Cilento, Pioppi, where he observed more the diet of the local people: he noticed farmers in villages of Southern Italy who were low on fat diets of animal origin and above all was made of bread and pasta or soup, along with with farm vegetables, legumes,fruits, olive oil, cheese, and wine. These practices, both for the farmers of Cilento and the inhabitants of the island of Crete, resulted in higher longevity and lower incidence of cardiovascular diseases than those observed in the citizens of Northern Europe and the United States. of America.

Benefits of the Mediterranean Diet

The Mediterranean diet which is characterized by low-fat content, mostly unsaturated, and by high intake of antioxidants, plays an important role in the prevention of cardiovascular diseases and other pathologies such as cancer, obesity, diabetes, osteoporosis, and mental problems.
The beneficial effects of this diet are associated with many factors, such as the richness of low-calorie foods, which help to maintain a healthy weight and ensure the use of fiber that prevents chronic diseases.

The Mediterranean diet is effective in maintaining good overall health and reduces the incidence of:

A. Bowel cancer
B. Breast neoplasia
C. Diabetes
D. Infarction
E. Atherosclerosis
F. Hypertension
G. Digestive diseases
H. Metabolic syndrome

Clean Fifteen and Dirty Dozen Lists for 2022

Here's the Environmental Working Group's annual guide, which includes Dirty Dozen and Clean lists of non-organic fruits with the most and least pesticides:

Dirty Dozen

- Strawberries
- Spinach
- Kale, cabbage, and mustard greens
- nectarines
- Apples
- Grapes
- Bell and hot peppers
- Cherries
- Peaches
- Pears
- Celery
- Tomatoes

Clean Fifteen

- Lawyers
- Sweet corn
- Pineapple
- Onions
- Papaya
- Frozen Peas
- asparagus
- Honeydew melon
- Kiwi
- Cabbage
- Mushrooms
- Cantaloupe
- Mangoes
- Watermelon
- Sweet potatoes

BREAKFAST

1. Pork Cracklings With Eggs

Total Prep Time: 10 Minutes | Total Cook Time: 10 Minutes | Makes: 3 Servings

INGREDIENTS

- 4 slices Bacon, cooked
- 5 Eggs
- 5 oz. Pork Rinds
- 1 Tomato
- 1/4 cup Cilantro, chopped

- 1 Avocado
- 2 Jalapeño Peppers, de-seeded
- 1 Onion
- Salt and Pepper to Taste

DIRECTIONS

1. In the bacon fat, fry pork rinds.
2. Add the vegetables to the skillet once the pig rinds are crispy.
3. Add chopped cilantro to the pan once the onions are almost transparent.
4. Mix everything in the pan with 5 pre-scrambled eggs.
5. Season with salt and pepper as needed.
6. Cook like an omelet.
7. Just before serving, dice an avocado and fold it into the mixture.

NUTRITION

Calories 421, 43g Fats, 5g Carbohydrates, 27g Protein.

2. <u>Italian pizza waffles</u>

Total Prep Time: 10 Minutes | Total Cook Time: 4 Minutes | Makes: 2 Servings

INGREDIENTS
- 4 Eggs
- 1 teaspoon Italian Seasoning
- 4 tablespoons Parmesan Cheese
- 3 tablespoons Almond Flour
- 1 tablespoon Bacon Grease
- 1 tablespoon Psyllium Husk Powder
- Salt and Pepper to Taste
- 1/2 cup Tomato Sauce
- 1 teaspoon Baking Powder
- 3 oz. Cheddar Cheese
- 14 slices Pepperoni

DIRECTIONS
1. In a container, combine all ingredients, excluding tomato sauce and cheese, using an immersion blender.
2. Preheat your waffle iron and pour half of the batter into it.
3. Allow cooking for a few minutes.
4. Top each waffle with tomato sauce and cheese.
5. Then, in the oven, broil for 4 minutes.
6. Add pepperoni on the top of them if desired.

NUTRITION
Calories: 526, 45g Fats, 5g Carbohydrates, 29g Protein

3. <u>Nutmeg-Spiced Quinoa porridge</u>

Total Prep Time: 10 Minutes | Total Cook Time: 15 Minutes | Makes: 4 Servings

INGREDIENTS:

- Pinch of ground cloves
- 2 cups of water
- 1 cup uncooked red quinoa, cooked
- ½ teaspoon ground ginger
- ½ teaspoon vanilla extract
- ½ cup coconut milk

- ¼ teaspoon fresh lemon zest, finely grated
- 10-12 drops of liquid stevia
- 1 teaspoon ground cinnamon
- ½ teaspoon ground nutmeg
- 2 tablespoons almonds, chopped

DIRECTIONS:
1. Combine quinoa and vanilla extract.
2. Add the coconut milk, lemon zest, stevia, and spices to the skillet with the quinoa and stir.
3. Fluff quinoa with a fork.
4. Divide the quinoa mixture evenly among serving bowls.
5. Serve with a garnish of chopped almonds.

NUTRITION
Calories: 248 | Fat: 11.4g | Carbs: 30.5g | Fiber: 4.4g| Sugars: 1.3g | Protein: 7.4g

4. <u>Protein Almond Muesli</u>

Total Prep Time: 10 Minutes | Makes: 2 Servings

INGREDIENTS:

- 1/2 teaspoon cinnamon
- 1 tablespoon raw almonds
- 1 cup unsweetened unsulfured coconut flakes
- 1 tablespoon chopped walnuts
- 1 tablespoon dark no-sugar-added chocolate chips
- 1 cup unsweetened almond milk
- 1 scoop of hemp protein

DIRECTIONS:

1. Toss together the coconut flakes, walnuts, almonds, and chocolate chips in a medium mixing dish.
2. Sprinkle cinnamon on top.
3. Douse the muesli with cold almond milk and devour with a spoon.

NUTRITION

Calories: 399 | Fat 8.20g | Carbohydrates 64.50g | Sugar 11.30g | Fibre 6.6g | Protein 20.30g

5. Apple Cinnamon Chia

Total Prep Time: 10 Minutes | Makes: 2 Servings

INGREDIENTS:

- 1/2 chopped dried apple
- 2 cups chia seeds
- 1 cup hemp hearts
- 2 tablespoons real cinnamon
- 1 teaspoon low sodium salt
- 1/2c chopped nuts of your choice

DIRECTIONS:

1. Combine all of the ingredients.
2. Add a few drops of stevia to each serving.

NUTRITION

Calories: 233 | protein 4.8g | carbohydrates 27.7g | dietary fiber10.1g | sugars 14.4g | fat 12.7g | saturated fat 1.1g

6. Apple Almond Coconut Bowl

Total Prep Time: 10 Minutes | Makes: 2 Servings

INGREDIENTS:

- Pinch of cinnamon
- one-half apple cored and roughly diced
- a handful of sliced almonds
- a handful of unsweetened coconut
- 1 pinch of low sodium salt

DIRECTIONS:

1. Combine all of the ingredients.
2. Add a few drops of stevia to each serving.

NUTRITION

Calories 160 | Total Fat 12g | Saturated fat 4.5g | Sodium 60mg | Potassium 144mg | Carbohydrates 12g | Sugar 8g | Fiber 3g | Protein 3g

7. Pecan Porridge with Banana

Total Prep Time: 10 Minutes | Makes: 2 Servings

INGREDIENTS

- ½ cup soaked pecans
- ¾ cup boiling water
- ½ very ripe banana
- a few drops of a few drops of stevia
- 2 tablespoons coconut butter
- ½ teaspoon cinnamon
- ⅛ teaspoon sea salt

DIRECTIONS

1. Blend everything until smooth and creamy.
2. Cook the mixture in a pan, about 5 minutes.

NUTRITION

Calories Per Serving: 290 | Total Fat 19g | Cholesterol 0mg | Sodium 10mg | Total Carbohydrates 28g | Sugars 18g | Protein 6g

8. Spicy Sweet potato Breakfast Bowl

Total Prep Time: 10 Minutes | Total Cook Time: 26 Minutes | Makes: 4 Servings

INGREDIENTS

- 2 sweet potatoes, peeled and diced
- Pinch Salt and pepper
- 1/2 bell pepper, diced
- 1 teaspoon chili powder
- 1/2 onion, diced
- Extra virgin olive oil
- 1 jalapeño, chopped
- 2-3 cups fresh spinach
- 2 eggs
- 1/2 red bell pepper, diced
- 1 avocado, sliced
- 1 teaspoon ghee
- 2 strips bacon, cooked and crumbled

DIRECTIONS

1. Preheat the oven to 375 degrees Fahrenheit.
2. Toss diced sweet potatoes with olive oil, salt, pepper, and chili powder on a lined baking pan.
3. Bake for 20 minutes, rotating halfway through.
4. Sauté the onion, bell peppers, and jalapeño in a skillet for 6 minutes, or until tender.
5. Add the spinach and cook.
6. In a separate skillet, melt the ghee. Cook until the eggs, seasoning with salt and pepper.
7. Place the sweet potatoes in two separate dishes.
8. Top with vegetable mixture, followed by the egg, bacon, and avocado.

NUTRITION

Calories 460 | Fat 23g grams | Saturated Fat 9g grams | Sodium 1000mg milligrams | Carbohydrates 24g grams | Fiber 4g grams | Sugars 7g grams | Protein 40g grams

9. Blueberry Cinnamon Breakfast Bake

Total Prep Time: 10 Minutes | Total Cook Time: 28 Minutes | Makes: 2 Servings

SERVINGS: 6 SERVINGS

INGREDIENTS:
- 2 teaspoons cinnamon, divided
- 2 eggs, beaten
- 1/4 cup brown sugar, divided
- 8 slices of whole-wheat bread
- 1 cup of low-fat milk
- 3 cups blueberries
- Zest of 1 lemon, divided

DIRECTIONS:
1. Preheat the oven to 350 degrees Fahrenheit (180 degrees Celsius).
2. Mix cinnamon, eggs, milk, brown sugar, and zest in a bowl.
3. In a mixing bowl, toss the bread and blueberries with the egg mixture and whisk until most of the liquid has been absorbed.
4. Pour batter into muffin tins.
5. Sprinkle 1 tablespoon brown sugar and 1 teaspoon cinnamon over the French toast cups.
6. Cook for 18 minutes, or until the French toast is done and the top is browned.
7. In a small saucepan, combine the remaining 1 cup of blueberries, lemon zest, and 1 tablespoon brown sugar and cook for 10 minutes, or until liquid is released.
8. Crush blueberries and dollop the syrupy blueberry over the toasted French toast.

NUTRITION
Calories: 170, 3g Fat, 171mg Sodium, 30g Carbohydrates (4g fiber, 15g Sugar, 7g Added), 7g Protein

10. Cinnamon quinoa with peach & Pecan

Total Prep Time: 10 Minutes | Total Cook Time: 2 Hours | Makes: 6 Servings

INGREDIENTS:
- Cooking spray
- 2 ½ cups water
- ½ teaspoon ground cinnamon
- 2 cups frozen, unsweetened peach slices
- 1 ½ cups fat-free half-and-half
- 1 cup uncooked quinoa, rinsed, drained
- ¼ cup sugar
- 1½ teaspoons vanilla extract
- ¼ cup chopped pecans, dry-roasted

DIRECTIONS
1. Add some water to a oiled slow cooker. .
2. In a mixing dish, combine the quinoa and cinnamon.
3. Cook for 2 hours on low, or until the quinoa is mushy and the water has been absorbed.
4. Just before serving the quinoa, mix the half-and-half, sugar, and vanilla essence in a separate dish until the sugar has dissolved.
5. Place the quinoa into dishes to serve. On top of that, place the peaches. Mix the half-and-half and pour it in.
6. Garnish with pecans.

NUTRITION
Calories: 249, Fat: 7 g, Saturated Fat: .5 g, Sodium: 65 Mg, Carbohydrate: 42 g, Protein: 10 g

11. <u>Cinnamon Chia Pudding</u>

Total Prep Time: 10 Minutes | Makes: 4 Servings

INGREDIENTS:

- 1/3 cup chia seeds
- 1½ cups almond milk
- ½ cup pumpkin purée
- pinch of salt
- 2 tablespoons of raw honey
- 1/8 teaspoon cloves
- 2 tablespoons almond butter
- 1 teaspoon vanilla extract
- 1 protein powder sachet
- ¼ teaspoon nutmeg powder
- 1 teaspoon cinnamon powder
- 1/8 teaspoon ginger

DIRECTIONS:

1. Blend everything, except the chia seeds.
2. Add the chia seeds and mix well.
3. Refrigerate overnight before serving.

NUTRITION

Calories: 363 | Fat: 29g | Carbs: 22.3g | Fiber: 6.6g | Sugars: 13.4g | Protein: 11.2g

12. <u>Walnut and almond porridge</u>

Total Prep Time: 15 Minutes | Total Cook Time: 25 Minutes | Makes: 5 Servings

INGREDIENTS:

- ½ cup pecans
- ½ cup almonds
- ¼ cup sunflower seeds
- ¼ cup chia seeds
- ¼ cup coconut flakes(unsweetened)
- 4 cups almond milk(unsweetened)
- ½ teaspoon cinnamon powder
- ¼ teaspoon ginger powder

- 1 teaspoon powdered stevia
- 1 tablespoon almond butter

DIRECTIONS:
1. In a food processor, combine pecans, almonds, and sunflower seeds.
2. Bring the nut mixture, chia seeds, coconut flakes, almond milk, spices, and stevia powder to a boil for about 20 minutes.
3. Serve with a dollop of almond butter.

NUTRITION
Calories: 292 | Fat: 7.5g | Carbs: 9.6g | Fiber: 6.5g | Sugars: 1.2g | Protein: 8g

13. <u>Cinnamon Millet porridge</u>

Total Prep Time: 10 Minutes | Total Cook Time: 10 Minutes | Makes: 4 Servings

INGREDIENTS:
- 2 teaspoons ground cinnamon
- ½ teaspoon ground cloves
- 1 tablespoon coconut butter
- 1½ cups finely ground millet
- 1½ cups of water
- 1 teaspoon ginger powder
- 4 cups unsweetened coconut milk

DIRECTIONS:
1. In a skillet over medium-high heat, melt the coconut oil and brown the spices for about 30 seconds.
2. Add millet and stir to combine.
3. Bring the water and coconut milk to a boil, stirring constantly.
4. Simmer for about 15 minutes.
5. Serve with desired garnish.

NUTRITION
Calories: 398 | Fat: 11.7g | Carbs: 63.1g | Fiber: 7.1g | Sugars: 6.1g | Protein: 9.4g

14. Quick Oats with coconut milk

Total Prep Time: 10 Minutes| Total Cook Time: 3 Minutes| Makes: 2 Servings

INGREDIENTS:

- 2/3 cup unsweetened coconut milk
- ½ cup gluten-free quick-cooking rolled oats
- ½ teaspoon ground cinnamon
- ½ teaspoon ground turmeric
- ¼ teaspoon ground ginger

DIRECTIONS:

1. In a microwave-safe bowl, combine milk and oats and microwave on high for about 45 seconds.
2. Mix in the spices.
3. Microwave for 2 minutes, stirring after 20 seconds.

NUTRITION

Calories: 121| Fat: 3.2g | Carbs: 17.8g | Fiber: 3g | Sugars: 2.5g | Protein: 3.9g

SNACKS AND APPETIZERS

15. <u>Neapolitan bombs</u>

Total Prep Time: 2 Hours | Makes: 24 bombs

INGREDIENTS
- 1/2 cup butter
- 1/2 cup Cream Cheese
- 2 tablespoons Erythritol
- 1/2 cup Coconut Oil
- 2 Strawberries
- 25 drops of Liquid Stevia
- 2 tablespoons Cocoa Powder
- 1 teaspoon Vanilla Extract
- 1/2 cup Sour Cream

DIRECTIONS
1. Blend the the butter, coconut oil, sour cream, cream cheese, erythritol, and stevia in an immersion blender until smooth.
2. Separate the mixture into three bowls. Toss the cocoa powder in one bowl, the strawberries in another, and the vanilla in the third.
3. Using an immersion blender, combine all of the ingredients once more. Pour the chocolate mixture into a spout-equipped container.
4. Fill a fat bomb mold halfway with the chocolate mixture. Freeze for 30 minutes before repeating with the vanilla mixture.
5. Freeze for at least 30 minutes.
6. Remove them from the fat bomb molds once they've totally frozen.

NUTRITION
102 Calories, 9g Fats, 0.4g Carbohydrates, and 0.6g Protein.

16. <u>Coconut orange creamsicle bombs</u>

Total Prep Time: 2 Hours | Makes: 10 Servings

INGREDIENTS

- 1/2 cup Coconut Oil
- 3 drops Liquid Stevia
- 4 oz. Cream Cheese
- 1/2 cup Heavy Whipping Cream
- 1 teaspoon Orange Vanilla Mio

DIRECTIONS

1. Combine the coconut oil, heavy cream, and cream cheese in a mixing bowl.
2. To combine all of the ingredients, use an immersion blender.
3. Combine the Vanilla Mio and stevia.
4. Freeze the mixture for 2 hours on a silicone dish.
5. Remove off the silicone tray once it has firm and place in the freezer.

NUTRITION

172 Calories, 20g Fats, 0.7g Carbohydrates, 1g Protein.

17. <u>Rotisserie chicken pizza</u>

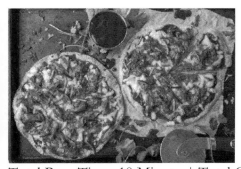

Total Prep Time: 10 Minutes | Total Cook Time: 13 Minutes | Makes: 4 Servings

INGREDIENTS
DAIRY-FREE PIZZA CRUST

- 6 Eggs
- 6 tablespoons Parmesan Cheese, shredded
- 3 tablespoons Psyllium Husk Powder
- 1 1/2 teaspoon Italian Seasoning
- Salt and Pepper to Taste

TOPPINGS

- 4 oz. Cheddar Cheese, shredded
- 6 oz. Rotisserie Chicken, shredded
- 4 tablespoons Tomato Sauce
- 1 tablespoons Mayonnaise
- 4 tablespoons BBQ Sauce

DIRECTIONS

1. Preheat the oven to 425 degrees Fahrenheit.
2. Blend the crust ingredients.
3. Using a silicone spatula, spread the dough out on a Silpat.
4. Bake crust for 10 minutes.
5. Flip the pizza once it's finished in the oven.
6. Add your chosen toppings and bake for another 3 minutes under the broiler.

NUTRITION

356 Calories, 25g Fats, 9g Carbohydrates, 25g Protein.

18. Olive Pizza bombs

Total Prep Time: 10 Minutes | Makes: 2 Servings

INGREDIENTS

- 4 oz. Cream Cheese
- 4 slices Pepperoni, diced
- 4 pitted Black Olives, diced
- 2 tablespoons Sun-Dried Tomato Pesto

DIRECTIONS

1. Combine basil, tomato pesto, and cream cheese in a mixing bowl.
2. Mix in the olives and pepperoni.
3. Form into balls and garnish with pepperoni, basil, and olives.

NUTRITION

110 Calories, 5g Fats, 3g Carbohydrates, 3g Protein.

19. Cocoa peanut butter bombs

Total Prep Time: 20 Minutes | Makes: 8 bombs

INGREDIENTS

- 2 tablespoons PB Fit Powder
- 1/4 cup Cocoa Powder
- 2 tablespoons Shelled Hemp Seeds
- 28 drops of Liquid Stevia
- 2 tablespoons Heavy Cream
- 1 teaspoon Vanilla Extract
- 1/2 cup Coconut Oil
- 1/4 cup Unsweetened Shredded Coconut

DIRECTIONS

1. Mix the dry ingredients with the coconut oil.
2. Combine the heavy cream, vanilla, and liquid stevia in a mixing bowl. Remix until everything is well incorporated and the texture is somewhat creamy.
3. On a plate, pour unsweetened shredded coconut
4. Roll the balls in your palm, then roll in coconut.
5. Place on a lined baking tray and freeze for 20 minutes.

NUTRITION

207 Calories, 20g Fats, 0.8g Carbohydrates, 4g Protein.

20. Mediterranean Edamame

Total Prep Time: 10 Minutes| Total Cook Time: 30 Minutes | Makes: 4 Servings

INGREDIENTS

- 1 yellow onion, minced
- 4 shiitake mushroom caps, sliced
- 10 ounces firm tofu, crumbled
- 1 tablespoon toasted sesame oil
- 1 teaspoon grated fresh ginger
- 1 cup shelled edamame, cooked in salted water until soft

- 2 green onions, minced
- 1 tablespoon toasted sesame seeds
- 2 tablespoons soy sauce
- 3 cups brown rice, cooked
- 1 tablespoon canola oil

DIRECTIONS

1. Heat the canola oil in a skillet; Sauté the onion, about 5 minutes.
2. Add mushrooms and cook for another 5 minutes.
3. Add the ginger and green onions.
4. Add tofu and soy sauce and combine thoroughly for about 5 minutes.
5. Add the edamame and cook, stirring frequently.
6. Distribute the hot rice among four bowls, then top with the edamame and tofu combination and sesame oil.
7. Serve garnished with sesame seeds.

NUTRITION

Calories: 167|Fat: 5g|Saturated: 1g|Carbohydrate: 23g|Fiber: 3g|Protein: 6g

21. Tortilla chips

Total Prep Time: 10 Minutes | Total Cook Time: 5 Minutes | Makes: 6 Servings

INGREDIENTS
TORTILLA CHIPS
- Flaxseed Tortillas
- Oil for Deep Frying

TOPPINGS
- Fresh Salsa
- Full-Fat Sour Cream

- Salt and Pepper to Taste

- Diced Jalapeño
- Shredded Cheese

DIRECTIONS
1. Preheat the deep fryer to 350°F.
2. Fry tortilla for 2 minutes per side.
3. Remove from the fryer and set aside to cool on paper towels.
4. Season well and serve with toppings.

NUTRITION
1g Fats, 0.04g Carbohydrates 0g, 0.9g Protein.

22. Jalapeño popper bombs

Total Prep Time: 10 Minutes | Makes: 2 Servings

INGREDIENTS
- 1/4 teaspoon Onion Powder
- 1/2 teaspoon Dried Parsley
- 3 oz. Cream Cheese
- 3 slices Bacon, cooked crisp

- 1/4 teaspoon Garlic Powder
- 1 Jalapeño Pepper, sliced
- Salt and Pepper to Taste

DIRECTIONS

1. Mix the cream cheese, jalapeño, spices, salt and pepper.
2. Mix in the bacon grease until it forms a firm consistency.
3. Place crumbled bacon on a platter.
4. Form into balls, then roll the balls in bacon.

NUTRITION

200 Calories, 13g Fats, 5g Net Carb, 8g Protein.

23. Low-Carb pan pizza dip

Total Prep Time: 10 Minutes | Total Cook Time: 20 Minutes | Makes: 1 Serving

INGREDIENTS

- 6 oz. Cream Cheese microwaved
- 1/4 cup Sour Cream
- 1/2 cup Mozzarella Cheese, shredded
- Salt and Pepper to Taste

- 1/4 cup Mayonnaise
- 1/2 cup Mozzarella Cheese, shredded
- 1/2 cup Low-Carb Tomato Sauce
- 1/4 cup Parmesan Cheese

DIRECTIONS

1. Preheat the oven to 350 degrees Fahrenheit.
2. Mix the cream cheese, sour cream, mayonnaise, mozzarella, salt and pepper.
3. Pour into ramekins and spread Tomato Sauce over each ramekin as well as mozzarella cheese and parmesan cheese.
4. Top your pan pizza dips with your favorite toppings.
5. Bake for 20 minutes.
6. Serve alongside some tasty breadsticks or pork rinds!

NUTRITION

349 Calories, 35g Fats, 4g Carbohydrates, 14g Protein.

24. <u>Corndog Muffins</u>

Total Prep Time: 10 Minutes | Total Cook Time: 15 Minutes | Makes: 10 Servings

INGREDIENTS
- 3 tablespoons Swerve Sweetener
- 1/2 cup Blanched Almond Flour
- 1/2 cup Flaxseed Meal
- 10 Smokies, halved
- 1/4 teaspoon salt
- 1 tablespoon Psyllium Husk Powder
- 1/4 cup butter, melted
- 1 Egg
- 1/3 cup Sour Cream
- 1/4 teaspoon Baking Powder
- 1/4 cup Coconut Milk

DIRECTIONS
1. Preheat the oven to 375 degrees Fahrenheit.
2. Mix all of the dry ingredients.
3. Mix in the egg, sour cream, and butter until thoroughly combined.
4. Mix in the coconut milk.
5. Place smokies in the center of the batter.
6. Bake for 12 minutes, then broil for 2 minutes.
7. Allow the muffins to cool in the tray for a few minutes before removing them to cool on a wire rack.
8. Serve with spring onion as a garnish.

NUTRITION
77 Calories, 8g Fats, 0.7g Carbohydrates, 4.1g Protein.

25. <u>Mediterranean Fried Queso Blanco</u>

Total Prep Time: 10 Minutes | Total Cook Time: 20 Minutes | Makes: 1 Serving

INGREDIENTS
- 6 oz. Queso Blanco, cubed
- 1 1/2 tablespoons Olive Oil
- 2 oz. Olives
- Pinch Red Pepper Flakes

DIRECTIONS
1. Heat the oil and melt the cheese cubes.
2. Continue to heat the cheese, then fold half of it in on itself.
3. Continue to flip the cheese and heat it until a beautiful crust forms.
4. Form a block with the melted cheese and seal all of the corners with another spatula, fork, or knife.
5. Remove the pan from the heat.
6. Cut into cubes and serve with olive oil and a sprinkle of pepper flakes.

NUTRITION
520 Calories, 43g Fats, 2g Carbohydrates, 30g Protein.

26. Cheddar and Bell pepper pizza

Total Prep Time: 10 Minutes | Total Cook Time: 20 Minutes | Makes: 2 Servings

INGREDIENTS
- Pizza dough
- 4 oz. Shredded Cheddar Cheese
- 1 Vine Tomato
- 1/4 cup Tomato Sauce
- 2/3 Bell Pepper
- 2-3 tablespoons Fresh Basil

DIRECTIONS
1. Preheat the oven to 350°F.
2. Bake the dough for about 8 minutes.
3. Slice vine tomato and place on each pizza dough, along with 2 tablespoons tomato sauce.
4. Top with shredded Cheddar cheese and bell peppers and bake another 10 minutes.
5. Serve garnished with fresh basil.

NUTRITION
410 Calories, 33g Fats, 3g Carbohydrates, and 28g Protein.

27. <u>Mediterranean Low-Sugar flat-bread pizza</u>

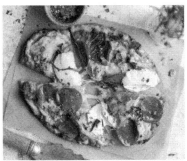

Total Prep Time: 10 Minutes | Total Cook Time: 22 Minutes | Makes: 2 Servings

INGREDIENTS
PEANUT SAUCE

- 4 tablespoons PBFit
- 2 tablespoons Rice Wine Vinegar
- 4 tablespoons Coconut Oil
- 4 tablespoons Reduced Sugar Ketchup

- 1 teaspoon Fish Sauce
- 4 tablespoons Soy Sauce
- Juice of 1/2 Lime
- Pizza Base

TOPPINGS

- 2 Chicken Thighs, cooked
- 3 oz. Mung Bean Sprouts
- 6 oz. Mozzarella Cheese
- 2 Green Onions

- 1 1/2 oz. Shredded Carrot
- 2 tablespoons Peanuts, chopped
- 3 tablespoons Cilantro, chopped

DIRECTIONS

1. Preheat the oven to 400 degrees Fahrenheit.
2. Blend the sauce ingredients.
3. Mix the egg into the cheese thoroughly. Then, completely combine the dry ingredients with the cheese.
4. Place the pizza base on a Silpat and press it from edge to edge to make a huge rectangle.
5. Bake for 14 minutes until browned.
6. Set aside the pre-cooked chicken, which has been chopped into bite-size parts.
7. Turn the pizza over and top with sauce, chicken, shredded carrots, and mozzarella; bake for another 8 minutes.
8. Garnish with mung bean sprouts, sliced spring onion, chopped peanuts, and cilantro.

NUTRITION

268 Calories, 21g Fats, 2g Carbohydrates, and 15g Protein.

28. <u>Ham and Cheese Stromboli</u>

Total Prep Time: 10 Minutes | Total Cook Time: 20 Minutes | Makes: 4 Servings

INGREDIENTS

- 4 tablespoons Almond Flour
- 3 tablespoons Coconut Flour
- 2 cups Mozzarella Cheese, shredded
- 1 Egg
- 5 oz. Cheddar Cheese
- 4 oz. Ham
- 1 teaspoon Italian Seasoning
- Salt and Pepper to Taste

DIRECTIONS

1. Mix almond, coconut flour, and seasonings.
2. Start incorporating the melted mozzarella into your flour mixture.
3. Add your egg and stir everything together.
4. Transfer dough to a parchment paper and place another parchment paper on top; flatten it out with a rolling pin.
5. Cut diagonal lines from the edges of the dough to the center with a pizza cutter.
6. Alternate between ham and cheddar on the uncut dough stretch.
7. Then, one slice of dough at a time, lift it and place it on top of the filling, covering it completely.
8. Bake for 20 minutes.

NUTRITION

300 Calories, 28g Fats, 7g Carbohydrates, 26g Protein.

29. <u>Mini Portobello pizzas</u>

Total Prep Time: 10 Minutes | Total Cook Time: 12 Minutes | Makes: 4 Servings

INGREDIENTS

- 1 Vine Tomato, sliced thin
- 1/4 Cup Fresh Chopped Basil
- Pinch Salt and Pepper
- 4 oz. Mozzarella Cheese
- 20 slices Pepperoni
- 6 tablespoons Olive Oil
- 4 Portobello Mushroom Caps

DIRECTIONS

1. Scrape out all of the mushroom's insides.
2. Preheat the oven to high broil and brush the insides of the mushrooms with Olive Oil. Season with salt and pepper.
3. Broil the mushroom for 3 minutes.
4. Turn the mushrooms over and brush with Olive Oil, and season with salt and pepper.
5. Broil a further 4 minutes.
6. In each mushroom, place a tomato and basil leaf.
7. Top each mushroom with 5 pieces of pepperoni and fresh cubed mozzarella cheese.
8. Broil for another 2 minutes.

NUTRITION

320 Calories, 31g Fats, 8g Carbohydrates, 5g Protein.

30. <u>Tofu and Capers Pizza</u>

Total Prep Time: 10 Minutes | Total Cook Time: 15 Minutes | Makes: 4 Servings

INGREDIENTS

- 2 tablespoons olive oil
- 16-ounce package of tofu, drained and sliced
- Pinch Salt
- 3 garlic cloves, minced
- 14.5-ounce can of diced tomatoes, drained
- ¼ cup sun-dried tomatoes, sliced
- 1 tablespoon capers
- 1 teaspoon dried oregano
- ½ teaspoon sugar
- Freshly ground black pepper
- 2 tablespoons minced fresh parsley

DIRECTIONS

1. Preheat the oven to 275 degrees Fahrenheit.
2. Cook tofu in a oiled skillet until the tofu is browned.
3. Season with salt and pepper.
4. Heat the remaining oil and sauté garlic for 1 minute.
5. Add all tomatoes, olives, and capers.
6. Toss in the oregano, sugar, and salt, then season to taste with pepper.
7. Cook for around ten minutes.
8. Drizzle the sauce over the fried tofu slices and garnish with parsley. Serve right away.

NUTRITION

Calories 795.6, Fat 37.6 g, Cholesterol 166.2 mg, Sodium 1842.2 mg, Carbohydrates 73.2, Protein 4

31. <u>Cheesy Ramen Pizzas</u>

Total Prep Time: 10 Minutes| Total Cook Time: 30 Minutes | Makes: 4 Servings

INGREDIENTS
- 6 oz. ramen noodles, cooked

OTHER TOPPINGS
- 1/2 cup milk
- 4 black olives
- 1 egg, beaten
- 1 cup mushroom
- 1 can jalapeño slices
- 1 cup barbecue sauce

- 2 cups mozzarella cheese, grated
- 1/4 cup Parmesan cheese, grated
- 1 cup bell pepper
- 1 cup cooked chicken, chopped
- 1 teaspoon red pepper flakes
- 1/2 red onion, sliced thinly
- 11-ounce mandarin oranges drained well

DIRECTIONS
1. Preheat your oven to 350 degrees F.
2. Whisk together the egg, milk, and Parmesan cheese in a pan.
3. Stir in the noodles.
4. Cook for about 12 minutes in the oven.
5. Sprinkle the barbecue sauce over the noodles, then add the chicken, onions, and oranges.
6. Evenly sprinkle the mozzarella cheese on top.
7. Cook for around 15 minutes in the oven.

NUTRITION
Calories 577.9, Fat 27.6g, Cholesterol 133.1mg, Sodium1510.0mg, Carbohydrates 50.6g, Protein 31.9g

32. <u>Pizza Breadsticks</u>

Total Prep Time: 14 Minutes| Total Cook Time: 20 Minutes | Makes: 4 Servings

INGREDIENTS
BREADSTICK BASE

- 2 cups Mozzarella Cheese, melted
- 3/4 cup Almond Flour
- 1 tablespoon Psyllium Husk Powder
- 3 tablespoons Cream Cheese
- 1 Egg

- 1 teaspoon Baking Powder
- 2 tablespoons Italian Seasoning
- 1 teaspoon salt
- 1 teaspoon Pepper

EXTRA TOPPINGS

- 1 teaspoon Garlic Powder
- 3 oz. Cheddar Cheese

- 1 teaspoon Onion Powder
- 1/4 cup Parmesan Cheese

DIRECTIONS

1. Preheat the oven to 400 degrees Fahrenheit.
2. Whisk egg and cream cheese.
3. Mix dry ingredients in another bowl.
4. Mix the wet and dry ingredients along with the mozzarella cheese.
5. Knead the dough together with your hands. Set it on a Silpat.
6. Transfer the dough to foil so you can cut it with a pizza cutter.
7. Cut the dough into pieces and season it with salt and pepper.
8. Bake until crisp, for 14 minutes.

NUTRITION

Calories 722 Fat 39.1 g, Carbohydrates 66.6g, Protein 29.2 g, Cholesterol 76 mg, Sodium 1027 mg

33. Easy Peasy pizza

Total Prep Time: 10 Minutes| Total Cook Time: 20 Minutes | Makes: 2 Servings

INGREDIENTS
PIZZA CRUST
- 1 tablespoon Psyllium Husk Powder
- 2 Eggs
- 2 tablespoons Parmesan Cheese

- 1/2 teaspoon Italian Seasoning
- Salt to Taste
- 2 teaspoon Frying Oil

TOPPINGS
- 5 oz. Mozzarella Cheese
- 3 tablespoons Low-Carb Tomato Sauce

- 1 tablespoon Freshly Chopped
- Basil

DIRECTIONS
1. Preheat the broiler to high.
2. Mix all the dry ingredients.
3. Using your immersion blender, combine 2 eggs with the rest of the ingredients.
4. Heat 2 teaspoons of frying oil.
5. Spread out dough into the pan.
6. Flip once the edges look golden.
7. Cook for 50 seconds on the other side.
8. Brush low-carb tomato sauce over the pizza.
9. Top with cheese and broil for a few minutes.

NUTRITION
59 Calories, 35g Fats, 5g Carbohydrates, 27g Protein.

34. <u>Sweet Potato Chicken Dumplings</u>

Total Prep Time: 10 Minutes| Total Cook Time: 30 Minutes | Makes: 8 Servings

INGREDIENTS:

- 1 cup frozen peas
- 1/2 cup all-purpose flour, divided
- 3 cups cooked chicken breast, shredded
- 1 cup carrots, sliced
- 2 cloves garlic, minced
- 1 teaspoon baking soda
- 2 cups low-sodium chicken broth
- 1 teaspoon black pepper, divided

- 1 cup kale, stemmed and chopped
- 1 cup wheat flour
- 1 onion, chopped
- 1 tablespoon olive oil
- 1 cup buttermilk
- 1 cup green beans, halved
- 1 sweet potato, cooked, peeled, and mashed
- 1/8 teaspoon salt

DIRECTIONS:

1. In a skillet, heat the oil.
2. Sauté onions with carrots, green beans, peas, kale, garlic, and pepper for 8 minutes.
3. Cook for another 3 minutes after adding the flour.
4. Mix in the broth and bring to a boil.
5. Toss the vegetables and shredded chicken together. Evenly distribute the batter among the 16 muffin cups.
6. Combine the flours, baking soda, salt, and remaining pepper in a mixing basin.
7. Mix in the mashed sweet potato and buttermilk.
8. Transfer to muffin cups, then top with the chicken mixture.
9. Bake for 15 minutes until golden.

NUTRITION

188 Calories, 4g Fat (1g Saturated), 18mg, Sodium, 29g Carbohydrates (5g fiber, 5g Sugar), 13g Protein

LUNCH

35. Roman Tuna Salad

Total Prep Time: 10 Minutes | Makes: 2 Servings

INGREDIENTS:

- 1 Tablespoon lemon juice
- 2 ribs of celery, diced finely
- 1 clove of garlic, minced
- 3 Tablespoons parsley
- 2 Tablespoons of extra virgin olive oil
- 10 sun-dried tomatoes, softened in warm water and chopped
- 10 oz. can of tuna, flaked
- Pinch low sodium salt and pepper

DIRECTIONS:

1. Toss everything in a mixing bowl.
2. Enjoy.

NUTRITION

Calories: 326, 45g Fats, 5g Carbohydrates, 39g Protein

36. Leftover Turkey Taco Salad

Total Prep Time: 10 Minutes | Makes: 2 Servings

INGREDIENTS:

- 1 tablespoon coconut or olive oil
- 1/2 lbs. leftover turkey, cooked and chopped
- 1 1/2 tablespoons taco seasoning
- 1/4 cup water
- 1 tablespoon of rice vinegar
- Shredded lettuc

TACO SEASONING:

- 1 teaspoon of red pepper flakes
- 1 teaspoon garlic powder
- 2 teaspoons of paprika
- 1 teaspoon onion powder
- 1 teaspoon oregano
- 3 tablespoons of chili powder

- 2 teaspoons cumin
- 4 teaspoons of low sodium salt

TOPPINGS
- Red Onion
- Sliced Olives
- Tomatoes
- Avocado
- Bell Peppers
- Crushed Sweet Potato Chips

DIRECTIONS:
1. In a skillet, heat oil and add the chicken; cook until the liquid has evaporated, stirring in the water and taco seasoning.
2. Prepare all of your toppings by shredding, chopping, and dicing them.
3. Combine lettuce, toppings, chicken, remaining oil and vinegar dressing, and smashed chips in a salad bowl.

NUTRITION
Calories 292.5 | Total Fat 6.0 g | Saturated Fat 1.8 g | Sodium 1,198.7 mg | Potassium 634.2 mg | Total Carbohydrate 29.2 g | Dietary Fiber 7.2 g | Sugars 3.3 g | Protein 31.1 g

37. Farfalle Pasta with Mushrooms

Total Prep Time: 10 Minutes | Total Cook Time: 35 Minutes | Makes: 4 Servings

INGREDIENTS
- 1 lb. farfalle pasta, cooked
- Pinch salt and pepper to taste
- 2 zucchinis, quartered and sliced
- 8-ounce package of mushrooms, sliced
- 1/3 cup olive oil
- 1 clove of garlic, chopped
- 1 tablespoon paprika
- 1 tablespoon dried oregano
- 1/4 cup butter
- 1 onion, chopped
- 1 tomato, chopped

DIRECTIONS
1. Fry garlic, mushrooms, onion, and tomato in olive oil for 17 minutes.
2. Season with salt, pepper, paprika, and oregano.
3. Combine the vegetables and noodles in a mixing bowl.

NUTRITION
Calories 720 kcal, Carbohydrates 92.8 g, Cholesterol 31 mg, Fat 32.9 g, Protein 18.1 g, Sodium 490 mg

38. Tortellini Salad with Spinach

Total Prep Time: 20 Minutes | Total Cook Time: 40 Minutes | Makes: 2 Servings

INGREDIENTS

- 9-ounce package of spinach and cheese
- 1 jar tortellini, cooked
- 4-ounce jar pesto
- 1/4 cup halved, seeded, and sliced cucumber
- 1/4 cup halved cherry tomatoes
- 1/4 cup red onion, diced
- 1/2 Cup chopped mache

DIRECTIONS

1. Place the cucumbers, tomatoes, onions, tortellini, and mache on top of the pesto in the jar.
2. Serve your salad right immediately or keep it refrigerated until ready to eat.

NUTRITION

Calories 716 kcal, Fat 39g, Carbohydrates 66g, Protein 29 g, Sodium 1027 mg

39. Egg Noodles with Croutons

Total Prep Time: 5 Minutes | Total Cook Time: 20 Minutes | Makes: 4 Servings

INGREDIENTS

- 12 oz. egg noodles, cooked
- 1 pinch salt
- 1/2 cup unsalted butter
- 1/4 teaspoon pepper
- 2 slices of white bread, torn

DIRECTIONS

1. Heat the butter in a pan and cook the bread pieces until crisp.
2. Add salt and black pepper.
3. Combine the noodles and croutons in a serving bowl.

NUTRITION

Calories 565.3, Fat 27.2g, Cholesterol 132.8mg, Sodium 145.0mg, Carbohydrates 67.3g, Protein 13.3g

40. Snow Peas & Spaghetti

Total Prep Time: 20 Minutes | Total Cook Time: 40 Minutes | Makes: 6 Servings

INGREDIENTS
- 8 oz. spaghetti, cooked
- 1 lb. boneless skinless chicken breast
- 1 tablespoons cornstarch
- 2 cups fresh snow peas
- 4 tablespoons reduced-sodium soy sauce,
- 2 cups carrots, shredded
- 3 green onions, chopped
- 2 tablespoons sesame oil, divided
- 3/8 teaspoon ground ginger, minced
- 1/2 teaspoon crushed red pepper flakes
- 1 tablespoon canola oil
- 2 tablespoons white vinegar
- 1 tablespoon sugar

DIRECTIONS
1. Whisk the sesame oil, cornstarch, and half the soy sauce in a zip-top bag along with the chicken.
2. Shake the bag to coat it and press it to seal it.
3. Set it aside for 20 minutes to absorb the flavors.
4. Mix the vinegar, sugar, remaining soy sauce, and sesame oil.
5. Heat the canola oil in a skillet and cook chicken for 8 minutes; add in the carrots, peas, green onions, ginger, and pepper flakes.
6. Combine chicken, vinegar sauce, and pasta; cook for 2 minutes before serving.

NUTRITION
Calories 337.1, Fat 9.5g, Cholesterol 48.4mg, Sodium 477.5mg, Carbohydrates 38.9g, Protein 22

41. <u>Garlic and sesame noodles</u>

Total Prep Time: 5 Minutes | Total Cook Time: 10 Minutes | Makes: 4 Servings

INGREDIENTS:

- 1-pound brown rice spaghetti, cooked
- 1½ tablespoons toasted sesame oil
- 1 cup sliced green onions
- 7 garlic cloves, crushed
- ¼ cup soy sauce
- ¼ cup hazelnut sugar
- 2 tablespoons rice vinegar
- ½ teaspoon red pepper flakes
- Sesame seeds for garnish

DIRECTIONS:

1. Over low to medium heat, heat a skillet.
2. Pour in the sesame oil and once heated, stir in ¾ cup of green onions, garlic, and red pepper flakes.
3. Cook until garlic is lightly browned and fragrant, stirring frequently to avoid burning.
4. Add soy sauce, coconut sugar, and rice vinegar and stir to combine. Add the prepared, drained pasta and toss to coat with the sauce.
5. Cook for 2 minutes.
6. Serve topped with the remaining green onions and sesame seeds

NUTRITION

Calories: 305KCAL | Carbohydrates: 47g | Protein: 7.2g | Fat: 12.8g | Fiber: 2.5g

42. <u>Low Sodium Salad with Capers</u>

Total Prep Time: 10 Minutes | Makes: 2 Servings

INGREDIENTS:

- 5 cups of any salad greens

DRESSING:
- 1/2 cup olive oil
- 3 tablespoons lemon juice
- Pinch low sodium salt and pepper
- 1 tablespoon pure mustard powder
- 3 tablespoons capers, minced

DIRECTIONS:
1. Combine the oil, lemon juice, and mustard in a mixing bowl.
2. Add veggies and mix thoroughly.
3. Capers, low sodium salt, and pepper should be added now.
4. Serve.

NUTRITION

Calories: 366 |Fat 35g|Saturated fat: 4g |Unsaturated fat: 29g |Trans fat: 0g |Carbohydrates: 10g |Sugar: 3g |Sodium: 305mg |Fiber: 3g |Protein: 5g |Cholesterol: 8mg

43. <u>Mixed Green Salad with Beets</u>

Total Prep Time: 10 Minutes| Total Cook Time: 34 Minutes| Makes: 3 Servings

INGREDIENTS:
- 2 teaspoon honey
- 2 tablespoons raw sunflower seeds, toasted in butter
- 1/3 cup reduced-fat feta cheese, crumbled
- 2 medium beets, boiled until fork-tender, peeled and diced
- 1/8 teaspoon salt
- 1 orange, sliced
- 2 tablespoons calcium-fortified orange juice
- 1/8 teaspoon black pepper
- 1/4 cup olive oil
- 3 cups packed mixed salad greens

DIRECTIONS:
1. Combine garlic, orange juice, honey, salt, and pepper; whisk in the olive oil.
2. Combine beets, sunflower seeds, orange segments, mixed greens, and feta cheese in a large serving bowl.
3. Drizzle with the dressing.

NUTRITION

220 Calories, 16g Fat (3g Saturated), 8mg Cholesterol, 227mg Sodium, 14g Carbohydrates (3g fiber, 10g Sugar), 4g Protein

44. <u>Farro Salad with Sweet Pea Pesto</u>

Total Prep Time: 10 Minutes| Makes: 8 Servings

INGREDIENTS:

- 2 cups cherry or grape tomatoes
- 1/4 cup parmesan cheese
- 2 cups peas
- 1/2 cup low-sodium canned white beans
- 2 cloves garlic
- 1 teaspoon black pepper

- 1/4 cup olive oil
- 2 tablespoons sunflower seeds, Hulled
- 1 cup farro, cooked and cooled
- Zest of 1 lemon
- 1 bell pepper, diced

DIRECTIONS:

1. Pulse peas, parmesan, garlic, sunflower seeds, and pepper until the peas are finely minced; slowly drip in the olive oil.
2. Combine everything in a mixing dish.

NUTRITION

200 Calories, 10g Fat (2g Saturated), 2mg Cholesterol, 86mg Sodium, 23g Carbohydrates (5g fiber, 4g Sugar, 0g Added), 7g Protein

45. <u>Cheesy Lemon Quinoa Salad</u>

Total Prep Time: 10 Minutes| Makes: 4 Servings
INGREDIENTS:

- Juice of 1/2 lemon
- 2 cloves garlic, minced
- Pinch teaspoon salt
- 2 tablespoons olive oil
- 1 small yellow bell pepper, diced
- 1 teaspoon black pepper

- 1 cucumber diced
- 1 tablespoon dill, chopped
- 1 cup reduced-fat feta cheese, crumbled
- 1 cup quinoa, cooked
- 1 cup cherry tomatoes, quartered

DIRECTIONS:
1. Whisk olive oil, garlic, lemon juice, salt, and pepper.
2. Toss everything with the dressing.

NUTRITION
250 Calories, 9g Fat (4g Saturated), 17mg Cholesterol, 262mg Sodium, 33g Carbohydrates (5g fiber, 4g Sugar, 0g Added), 9g Protein

46. <u>Mediterranean Spinach and potatoes</u>

Total Prep Time: 10 Minutes | Total Cook Time: 1 hour 35 Minutes | Makes: 8 Servings

INGREDIENTS:
- 4 medium russet potatoes, washed
- 1 tablespoon oregano
- 1 tablespoon olive oil, extra-virgin
- 3 garlic cloves, crushed
- 1 teaspoon kosher salt
- ⅓ cup light cream cheese
- 1 cup onion, diced
- 1 teaspoon ground pepper
- 1-pound spinach, chopped
- 1 cup crumbled feta cheese

DIRECTIONS:
1. Preheat the oven to 400 degrees F.
2. Bake directly on the middle rack until tender, 50 to 60 minutes.
3. In a saucepan, heat the oil.
4. Add onion and cook until onion is soft, 3 minutes.
5. Add the spinach, garlic, and oregano.
6. Cook, stirring constantly, until the mixture is hot, about 4 minutes.
7. In a 9 x 13-inch skillet, arrange the potato skins.
8. Pulse the cream cheese, pepper, and salt using a hand blender.
9. Stir in spinach mixture and 1/2 cup feta. Fill each potato skin with about 3/4 cup filling. Sprinkle the remaining 1 tablespoon of feta on top.
10. Bake until topping is smoking and feta is golden brown, 25 to 35 minutes.

NUTRITION
197 Calories | Protein 7.8g | Carbohydrates 24.2g | Dietary Fiber 3.7g | Sugar 3.1 g | Fat 8.3g | Saturated Fat 4.3g

47. Mediterranean Fried spinach

Total Prep Time: 10 Minutes | Total Cook Time: 10 Minutes | Makes: 4 Servings

INGREDIENTS:
- 2 teaspoons olive oil (extra-virgin)
- ¼ cup currants
- Salt and freshly ground pepper to taste
- 1 small onion, diced
- 1 clove of garlic, minced
- 1 pound spinach leaves, sliced
- 3 tablespoons pine nuts, toasted
- Balsamic vinegar, to taste

DIRECTIONS:
1. Heat the oil and then cook the onion and garlic.
2. Add spinach and cook, tossing periodically until spinach is heated through.
3. Mix in pine nuts, balsamic vinegar, salt, currants,and pepper.

NUTRITION
117 calories | protein 5.3g | carbs 14.2g | dietary fiber 4.4g | sugar 8g | fat 5.9g | saturated fat 0.6g

48. Brussels, Carrot & Greens

Total Prep Time: 10 Minutes | Total Cook Time: 8 Minutes | Makes: 2 Servings

INGREDIENTS:
- 1 broccoli
- 2 carrots, sliced thin
- 6 brussels sprouts
- 2 cloves of garlic
- 1 teaspoon of caraway seeds
- 1/2 lemon
- Peel 1 lemon Olive oil

DIRECTIONS:

1. Steam all the vegetables for 8 minutes on low heat.
2. Sauté garlic with caraway seeds, lemon peel, lemon juice, and olive oil.
3. Add the carrot and Brussels sprouts.

NUTRITION

Calories 160| Fat 3g (Saturated 0g) | Cholesterol 0mg| Sodium 549mg| Carbohydrate 30g| Dietary Fiber 5g| Protein 8g.

49. <u>Split Peas with Spinach</u>

Total Prep Time: 10 Minutes| Total Cook Time: 2 Hours | Makes: 4 Servings

INGREDIENTS

- 2 plum tomatoes, chopped
- ½ teaspoon turmeric
- 1cup yellow split peas, rinsed and drained
- 1 serrano chile, seeded and minced
- 4 cups water
- 1 teaspoon salt
- 1 teaspoon ground cumin

- 2 cups fresh baby spinach
- ¼ cup chopped fresh cilantro
- 1 tablespoon canola oil
- 2 garlic cloves, minced
- 1 tablespoon ginger, finely chopped
- ½ teaspoon ground coriander
- 2 teaspoons fresh lemon juice

DIRECTIONS

1. Boil the split peas until soft, about 40 minutes.
2. Stir in the spinach, tomatoes; set aside.
3. Heat the oil in a skillet and cook the garlic, ginger, and chile for 1 minute.
4. Season with cumin, coriander, turmeric, and lemon juice.
5. Stir the mixture into the dal,
6. Serve.

NUTRITION

Calories: 215, Total Fat: 7 g (Saturated Fat: 1.0 g), Sodium: 128 Mg, Total Carbohydrate: 36 g (Dietary Fiber: 9 g, Sugar: 14 g), Protein: 7 g

50. <u>Stir-Fried Vegetables & Rice</u>

Total Prep Time: 10 Minutes | Total Cook Time: 15 Minutes | Makes: 4 Servings

INGREDIENTS

- 1 onion, chopped
- 1 carrot, chopped
- 2 teaspoons dry white wine
- 1 zucchini, chopped
- 2 tablespoons soy sauce
- 2 garlic cloves, minced
- ½ teaspoon turmeric

- 2 teaspoons grated fresh ginger
- 2 green onions, minced
- 2 tablespoons grape-seed oil
- 3 cups long-grain rice, cooked
- 1 cup peas
- 1 tablespoon toasted sesame oil

DIRECTIONS

1. Heat the oil in a skillet and sauté the onion, carrot, and zucchini for about 5 minutes.
2. Mix in the garlic, ginger, and green onions, about 3 minutes.
3. Stir in the rice, peas, soy sauce, and wine, for about 5 minutes.
4. Drizzle with sesame oil.

NUTRITION

Calories 160| Fat 3g (Saturated 0g) | Cholesterol 0mg| Sodium 549mg| Carbohydrate 30g| Dietary Fiber 5g| Protein
g

51. <u>Lemon Pasta with Broccoli</u>

Total Prep Time: 10 Minutes | Makes: 2 Servings

INGREDIENTS:

- 1 broccoli head
- Handful of peas
- Pinch Himalayan salt & black pepper
- 1 teaspoon of coconut oil
- 2 garlic cloves

- 2 Servings of Spelt pasta, cooked
- 1 courgette
- 1 tomato
- 1/2 red onion
- Juice of 1 lemon

- 2 bunches of rocket
- Drizzle of olive oil

DIRECTIONS:
1. Sauté the broccoli, peas, garlic, red onion, and courgette in coconut oil.
2. Toss in the pasta along with the chopped tomato and rocket, and the lemon juice.

NUTRITION
Calories 160| Fat 3g (Saturated 0g) | Cholesterol 0mg| Sodium 549mg| Carbohydrate 30g| Dietary Fiber 5g| Protein 8g

52. <u>Aubergine, Potato & Chickpea</u>

Total Prep Time: 10 Minutes| Total Cook Time: 10 Minutes | Makes: 2 Servings

INGREDIENTS:
- 1 onion, peeled and finely sliced
- 1 teaspoon coriander
- 1 aubergine
- 1 potato
- 2 tablespoons coconut oil
- 1/2 teaspoons cumin
- 1 can chickpeas
- 1/4 teaspoons turmeric
- Fresh coriander

SAUCE:
- 1 onion, peeled and finely sliced
- 2 teaspoons ginger, peeled and grated
- 1/2 teaspoons cumin
- 6 whole cloves
- 450g plum tomatoes
- 1/4 teaspoons turmeric
- 2 tablespoons coconut oil
- 3 cloves garlic, crushed
- 1 1/2 teaspoons salt
- 1 teaspoon red chili powder

DIRECTIONS:
1. Sauté onion and cumin seeds for 3 minutes.
2. Add the potato, aubergine, chickpeas, ground coriander, cumin, and turmeric.
3. Cook the onion, garlic, ginger, and cloves for sixty seconds and then add the chopped tomatoes, turmeric, and other spices.
4. Blend the sauces with a hand blender until they are roughly blended. After that, add the vegetables, coriander, water, salt, and pepper to taste.

NUTRITION
197 calories| Protein 7.8g| carbohydrates 24.2g | dietary fiber 3.7g | sugar 3.1 g | fat 8.3g | saturated fat 4.3g

53. <u>Kale Slaw & Creamy Dressing</u>

Total Prep Time: 15 Minutes| Makes: 2 Servings

INGREDIENTS:

- 1/3 cup sesame seeds
- 1 bell pepper
- 1/3 cup sunflower seeds
- 1 red onion
- 1 bunch of kale
- 4 cups of red cabbage, shredded
- 1 piece of root ginger
- Fresh coriander
- 1 Serving cashew dressing

DIRECTIONS:
1. Toss all the ingredients together.

NUTRITION
Calories 160| Fat 3g (Saturated 0g) | Cholesterol 0mg| Sodium 549mg| Carbohydrate 30g| Dietary Fiber 5g| Protein 8g

54. <u>Brussels, Carrot & Greens</u>

Total Prep Time: 10 Minutes| Total Cook Time: 10 Minutes | Makes: 4 Servings

INGREDIENTS:
- 1 broccoli
- 2 carrots, sliced thin
- 6 Brussels sprouts
- 2 cloves of garlic
- 1 teaspoon of caraway seeds
- 1/2 lemon
- Peel 1 lemon Olive oi

DIRECTIONS:
1. Steam all the vegetables for 7 minutes on low heat.
2. Sauté garlic with caraway seeds, lemon peel, 1/2 lemon juice, and olive oil.
3. Add the carrot and Brussels sprouts.

NUTRITION
Calories 160| Fat 3g (Saturated 0g) | Cholesterol 0mg| Sodium 549mg| Carbohydrate 30g| Dietary Fiber 5g| Protein 8g.

55. Broccoli Cauliflower Fry

Total Prep Time: 10 Minutes| Total Cook Time: 20 Minutes | Makes: 2 Servings

INGREDIENTS:
- 4 broccoli florets
- 4 cauliflower florets
- 1 pepper
- Handful assorted sprouts
- 3 spring onions
- 1 garlic clove, chopped Liquid Aminos
- Wild/brown rice

DIRECTIONS:
1. Cook the rice in a vegetable stock that is yeast-free.
2. Fry the garlic and onion in a steamer for three minutes.
3. Toss in the remaining ingredients and simmer for a few minutes more.

NUTRITION
197 calories| Protein 7.8g| carbohydrates 24.2g | dietary fiber 3.7g | sugar 3.1 g | fat 8.3g | saturated fat 4.3g

56. Asparagus and Zucchini Pasta

Total Prep Time: 10 Minutes| Total Cook Time: 10 Minutes | Makes: 4 Servings
INGREDIENTS:
- 1 zucchini
- 1 bunch asparagus, steamed
- 4 tomatoes, diced
- 200g of rocket
- 12 basil leaves
- 2 cloves garlic
- 1/2 red onion, diced
- 4 servings of spelt pasta, cooked

- Olive oil

DIRECTIONS:
1. Combine onion and tomatoes with handfuls of rocket, and asparagus and set them aside.
2. Blend remaining ingredients until a smooth, light green sauce forms.
3. Toss the pasta with the sauce, divide it into bowls, and top with the tomato, red onion, asparagus, and rocket.

NUTRITION
Calories 160| Fat 3g (Saturated 0g) | Cholesterol 0mg| Sodium 549mg| Carbohydrate 30g| Dietary Fiber 5g| Protein 8g.

57. Veggie-Stuffed Tomatoes

Total Prep Time: 10 Minutes| Total Cook Time: 10 Minutes | Makes: 4 Servings

INGREDIENTS:
- 1 tablespoon cold-pressed oil
- 2 tomatoes
- Half a small aubergine
- 1 onion
- 1/3 of a courgette
- 1-2 cloves of garlic
- Pinch of sea salt and pepper
- 1 bunch of fresh spinach leaves

DIRECTIONS:
1. Preheat the oven to 160 degrees Celsius (325 degrees Fahrenheit).
2. Toss vegetables with spinach, salt, and pepper, and oil.
3. After that, place the tomatoes on top and scoop out the center. Combine the middle piece with the rest of the mixture and stir well.
4. Now you must carefully place everything back into the tomatoes.
5. Put the tomatoes in a large pan with about 80ml of water and cover it with a lid once you're sure there's nothing else that could fit into them.
6. Bake for 18 minutes.

NUTRITION
Calories 160| Fat 3g (Saturated 0g) | Cholesterol 0mg| Sodium 549mg| Carbohydrate 30g| Dietary Fiber 5g| Protein 8g.

58. Mediterranean Ratatouille

Total Prep Time: 10 Minutes| Total Cook Time: 3 Minutes | Makes: 4 Servings

INGREDIENTS:
- 2 bunches of baby spinach
- 3 aubergines, skins removed and diced
- 6 Pitted black olives
- 3 courgettes, skins removed and diced
- 2 red peppers
- 5 tomatoes, diced
- 3 teaspoons thyme leaves
- 2 cloves of garlic
- Basil leaves
- Coriander seeds
- Drizzle extra virgin olive oil
- Pinch Himalayan salt & black pepper

DIRECTIONS:
1. In a skillet, heat a little olive or coconut oil and sauté one garlic bulb slowly.
2. Place the aubergine in a strainer and press with kitchen paper towels to remove any excess oil after cooking it all at once.
3. Heat more oil, then add the courgette and the other garlic.
4. Combine the remaining ingredients in a big pan and heat for 3 minutes.

NUTRITION
197 calories| Protein 7.8g| carbohydrates 24.2g | dietary fiber 3.7g | sugar 3.1 g | fat 8.3g | saturated fat 4.3g

59. Mango, Jalapeño & bean salad

Total Prep Time: 10 Minutes | Makes: 6 Servings

INGREDIENTS:

- 1 bell pepper, seeded, cut into ½-inch pieces
- 1 cup avocado, cubed
- 2 tablespoons lime juice
- 1 teaspoon salt
- 2 green onions, sliced
- 15-ounce can, of low-sodium whole kernel corn
- 1 teaspoon chili powder

- 1 jalapeño pepper, diced
- 15-ounce can black beans, drained
- 2 mangos, cut into ½-inch cubes
- 2 tablespoons fresh cilantro, chopped
- 1 tablespoon olive oil
- 1 teaspoon black pepper
- Shredded lettuce

DIRECTIONS

1. Divide lettuce among 6 plated.
2. Mix the black beans, corn, mango, avocado, onions, and jalapeño pepper.
3. Blend the lime juice, olive oil, cilantro, chili powder, black pepper, and salt in a jar with a secure lid and shake vigorously to combine. Pour the mango-avocado mixture on top.
4. Drizzle over lettuce and mixed greens, gently tossing to coat.

NUTRITION

Calories: 215, Total Fat: 7 g (Saturated Fat: 1.0 g), Sodium: 128 Mg, Total Carbohydrate: 36 g (Dietary Fiber: 9 g, Sugar: 14 g), Protein: 7 g

60. Spinach, Shrimp & Tangerine Bowl

Total Prep Time: 15 Minutes | Total Cook Time: 10 Minutes | Makes: 4 Servings

INGREDIENTS

- 1 cup endive
- 1 tablespoon parsley, chopped
- 1/4 small red onions, sliced in rings
- 3 cups spinach

- 1 tablespoon clarified butter
- 1/2 cup cooked shrimp (tails removed)
- 2 small tangerines, peeled and sectioned
- 1/4 cup roasted pine nuts

- 1 tablespoon basil, chopped
- 1 teaspoon fresh lime juice

DIRECTIONS
1. Combine the onion, spinach, endive, basil, and parsley in a large salad bowl.
2. Heat butter and cook the shrimp and lime together for one minute.
3. Toss the shrimp, pine nuts, and dressing of your choice into the salad bowl mix to combine.
4. Serve the salad with tangerine wedges as a garnish.

NUTRITION
Calories 239| Fat 22g (Saturated 5g) | Cholesterol 35mg| Sodium 48mg| Carbohydrate 7g| Dietary Fiber 2g| Protein 7g.

61. <u>Spicy Turkey Stir Fry</u>

Total Prep Time: 10 Minutes| Total Cook Time: 34 Minutes| Makes: 3 Servings

INGREDIENTS:
- 1 teaspoon garam masala
- 2 bell peppers, thinly sliced
- 2 tablespoons coconut oil
- Pinch low sodium salt

- 2 teaspoons freshly ground pepper
- 2 lbs. boneless skinless turkey breasts, sliced
- 1 teaspoon cumin seeds

FOR THE MARINADE:
- 1 teaspoon ginger, minced
- 1 clove of garlic, minced
- 1/2 cup coconut cream

- 1/4 teaspoon turmeric
- 1 teaspoon low sodium salt

DIRECTIONS:
1. Combine the marinade ingredients with the chicken and set aside for 1 hour.
2. In a wok or large sauté pan, melt the coconut oil over medium-high heat, then add the cumin seeds and cook for 3 minutes.
3. After adding the marinated chicken, cook for 5 minutes and then stir in the peppers, garam masala, and pepper.
4. Add a pinch of low-sodium salt to taste.
5. Cook for 5 minutes, stirring regularly.

NUTRITION
233 calories| 6g fat (1g saturated fat)|70mg cholesterol| 866mg sodium| 13g carbohydrate (0 sugars, 3g fiber)| 33g protein

62. <u>Roasted Lemon Herb Chicken</u>

Total Prep Time: 10 Minutes | Total Cook Time: 1 Hour | Makes: 4 Servings

INGREDIENTS:

- 1 medium onion, sliced thin
- 12 pieces of bone-in chicken thighs & legs
- 1 teaspoon dried thyme

FOR THE MARINADE:

- 2 drops of stevia
- 3 tablespoons extra virgin olive oil
- Pinch low sodium salt and freshly ground pepper
- 1 teaspoon onion powder
- Juice of 1 lemon

- 1 tablespoon dried rosemary
- 1 orange, sliced thin
- 1 lemon,

- 1 tablespoon Italian seasoning
- 3 cloves of garlic, minced
- Juice of 1 orange
- Dash of red pepper flakes

DIRECTIONS:

1. Mix all of the marinade ingredients with chicken in a baking dish.
2. Layer the onion, orange, and lemon slices on top of the chicken.
3. Season with thyme, rosemary, low sodium salt, and pepper.
4. Cover and bake for 30 minutes.
5. Uncover and bake for another 30 minutes.

NUTRITION

Calories: 405.3 | Protein: 32.2g | Carbohydrates: 3.6g | Dietary Fiber: 1.5g | Sugars: 0.1g | Fat: 29.2g | Saturated Fat: 7.8g | Cholesterol: 127.7mg | Iron: 2mg | Sodium: 177.6mg

63. <u>Basil Turkey with Roasted Tomatoes</u>

Total Prep Time: 10 Minutes | Total Cook Time: 1 Hour | Makes: 4 Servings

INGREDIENTS:

- 1/2 cup thinly sliced fresh basil
- 2 turkey breasts
- a few drops of stevia
- 1 cup mushrooms, chopped

- 1/2 medium onion, chopped
- 1 tablespoons extra virgin olive oil
- 1-pint cherry tomatoes
- Pinch low sodium salt and pepper

DIRECTIONS:

1. Drizzle olive oil and stevia over the tomatoes on a baking sheet.
2. Add salt and pepper.
3. Bake until soft, about 20 minutes.
4. Heat olive oil and cook onions and mushrooms for 10 minutes.
5. Add turkey and season with low sodium salt and pepper; cook for 15 minutes.
6. Serve the tomatoes followed by turkey breast and then the onions, mushrooms, and pan drippings.

NUTRITION

Calories 300 | Total Fat 14 g | Saturated Fat 6 g | Sodium 480 mg | Total Carbohydrate 23 g | Dietary Fiber 2 g | Sugars 3 g | Protein 26 g

64. <u>Sunflower Seed Pesto Chicken</u>

Total Prep Time: 10 Minutes | Total Cook Time: 20 Minutes | Makes: 4 Servings

INGREDIENTS:

PESTO

- 2 tablespoons parmesan cheese, grated
- 1 clove of garlic, chopped
- 2 tablespoons raw, hulled sunflower seeds
- 1/4 cup olive oil

- 1/8 teaspoon salt
- 1/8 teaspoon black pepper
- 1 cup basil leaves

CHICKEN AND GARNISHES

- 2 boneless, skinless chicken breasts, sliced lengthwise
- 1/4 cup part-skim mozzarella cheese, shredded and divided
- 2 tomatoes, sliced

DIRECTIONS:
1. Place the chicken on a rimmed baking sheet that has been oiled.
2. Blitz the pesto ingredients in a food processor.
3. Layer chicken with pesto, tomato slices, and mozzarella.
4. Bake for 15 minutes.

NUTRITION
244 Calories, 10g Fat (2g Saturated), 47mg Cholesterol, 314mg Sodium, 19g Carbohydrates (8g fiber, 11g Sugar, 0g Added), 25g Protein

65. Hearty Cauliflower Rice with chicken

Total Prep Time: 10 Minutes | Total Cook Time: 14 Minutes | Makes: 4 Servings

INGREDIENTS:
- 1 tablespoon honey
- 3 tablespoons oil
- 2 boneless, skinless chicken breasts, cubed
- 1 cup frozen peas and carrots, mixed
- 1 teaspoon turmeric powder
- 1 teaspoon fresh ginger, grated
- 3 cloves garlic, minced
- 1/4 teaspoon black pepper
- 2 tablespoons rice wine vinegar
- 3/4 cup orange juice
- 1 head cauliflower
- 3 scallions, sliced, whites & greens divided
- 1 tablespoon corn starch
- 1/2 red bell pepper, diced
- 1 1/2 tablespoons low-sodium soy sauce
- 2 large eggs, beate

DIRECTIONS:
1. Whisk orange juice, rice wine vinegar, soy sauce, honey, cornstarch, and ginger.
2. Scramble the eggs well.
3. Toss in the peas and carrots, scallion, garlic, and bell pepper with the remaining tablespoon of oil in the skillet, about 4 minutes.
4. Toss in the riced cauliflower, coated with cooking spray.
5. Cook for another 5 minutes, stirring regularly, or until cauliflower is somewhat crunchy.
6. In a skillet with the cauliflower, sauté the cooked chicken, eggs, veggies, and sauce until the sauce thickens, about 3 minutes.
7. Serve garnished with scallion greens.

NUTRITION
132 Calories, 3g Fat (1g Saturated), 90mg Cholesterol, 223mg Sodium, 14g Carbohydrates (3g fiber, 8g Sugar), 15g Protein

66. Black Pepper Salmon with yogurt

Total Prep Time: 10 Minutes| Total Cook Time: 14 Minutes | Makes: 4 Servings

INGREDIENTS:

YOGURT MARINADE

- ¼ teaspoon cayenne powder
- ¼ cup low-fat Greek yogurt
- ½ teaspoon coriander powder
- ½ teaspoon ginger powder
- ½ teaspoon turmeric powder
- Pinch Salt
- Pinch ground black pepper

SALMON

- 4 skinless salmon fillets

DIRECTIONS:

1. Heat the broiler.
2. Place the salmon fillets in a single layer on the broiler pan.
3. Spoon the yogurt mixture evenly over each fillet.
4. Grill for about 15 minutes.

NUTRITION

Calories: 313| Fat: 18.3g | Carbs: 1.4g | Fiber: 0.1g| Sugars: 1g | Protein: 34g

67. Arugula & pear salad with walnuts

Total Prep Time: 10 Minutes| Total Cook Time: 4 Minutes| Makes: 8 Servings

INGREDIENTS

SALAD

- 4 cups arugula, trimmed, washed, and dried
- 2 firm red Bartlett pears, cut into 16 wedges
- ½ cup walnuts, chopped and toasted
- 5 cups butter-head lettuce

DRESSING

- 2 tablespoons minced shallot
- ½ teaspoon Dijon mustard
- Pinch freshly ground pepper
- 3 tablespoons extra-virgin olive oil
- 3 tablespoons vegetable broth
- 1 ½ tablespoon balsamic vinegar

- ¼ teaspoon salt

DIRECTIONS
1. Whisk the shallot, broth, oil, vinegar, mustard, salt, and pepper.
2. Half-fill a big mixing bowl with water. Toss with 1 tablespoon of the dressing to coat.
3. In a mixing bowl, combine the lettuce, arugula, and remaining dressing.
4. Top with walnuts and serve.

NUTRITION
Calories: 125, Total Fat: 8 g (Saturated Fat: 1 g, Unsaturated Fat: 8 g), Cholesterol: 0 Mg Sodium: 104 Mg, Total Carbohydrates: 10 g (Fiber: 3 g, Sugar: 5 g), Protein: 2 g

68. <u>Mushrooms & spinach</u>

Total Prep Time: 15 Minutes | Total Cook Time: 15 Minutes | Makes: 3 Servings

INGREDIENTS:
- 1 teaspoon coconut oil
- 5-6 mushrooms, sliced
- 2 tablespoons olive oil
- 1 red onion, sliced
- 1 teaspoon fresh lemon zest, finely grated
- ¼ cup cherry tomatoes, sliced
- Pinch of ground nutmeg
- 3 cups fresh spinach, shredded
- 1 clove of garlic, minced
- ½ Tablespoons fresh lemon juice
- Pinch Salt
- Pinch ground black pepper

DIRECTIONS:
1. Heat the coconut oil and sauté the mushrooms for about 4 minutes.
2. Sauté the onion in olive oil and for about 3 minutes.
3. Add the garlic, lemon zest and tomatoes, salt, and black pepper and cook for about 2-3 minutes, lightly crushing the tomatoes with a spatula.
4. Cook for about 3 minutes with the spinach.
5. Stir in mushrooms and lemon juice and remove from heat.

NUTRITION
Calories: 179 | Fat: 16.8g | Carbs: 7.3g | Fiber: 2.4g | Sugars: 2.9g | Protein: 3.4g

69. <u>Creamy Baked Chicken</u>

Total Prep Time: 10 Minutes | Total Cook Time: 12 Minutes | Makes: 4 Servings

INGREDIENTS:
- 1/2 cup panko
- 1 tablespoon olive oil
- 2 medium boneless, skinless chicken breasts, sliced lengthways
- 1 teaspoon onion powder
- 1 teaspoon black pepper
- 1/3 cup Greek yogurt
- 1/2 cup shredded low-fat cheddar cheese
- 1 teaspoon garlic powder

DIRECTIONS:
1. Arrange your chicken on a well-oiled rimmed baking sheet.
2. Dredge with Greek yogurt.
3. Mix the dry ingredients in a small mixing bowl and sprinkle on top of the chicken.
4. Bake for 12 minutes at 425 degrees.

NUTRITION
193 Calories, 7g Fat (2g Saturated), 39mg Cholesterol, 363mg Sodium, 12g Carbohydrates (1g fiber, 2g Sugar, 1g Added), 20g Protein

70. <u>Seared Chicken & Tomatoes</u>

Total Prep Time: 10 Minutes | Total Cook Time: 15 Minutes | Makes: 4 Servings
INGREDIENTS:

- 2 chicken breasts, cut lengthwise
- 1 cup cherry tomatoes, quartered
- 3 cloves garlic, minced
- 1 cup quinoa
- 1 tablespoon dill
- 1 teaspoon black pepper
- Juice of 1 lemon
- 1 cup reduced-fat feta cheese, crumbled
- 1 tablespoon vegetable oil
- 1 bell pepper, diced
- 1 teaspoon salt
- 1 cucumber diced

DIRECTIONS:
1. Mix half the oil, garlic cloves, and basil with the chicken breasts in a zip-lock bag.
2. Bring the balsamic vinegar and honey to a boil.
3. In a small mixing dish, combine chopped tomatoes, remaining 2 garlic cloves, and 1/4 cup basil leaves; set aside.
4. In another pan, heat the remaining olive oil and brown chicken breasts for 3 minutes on each side.
5. Drizzle 1/4 cup tomato mixture and balsamic glaze over chicken breast halves.

NUTRITION
294 Calories,10g Fat (2g Saturated), 84mg Cholesterol, 88mg Sodium, 16g Carbohydrates (2g fiber, 12g Sugar, 4g Added), 32g Protein

71. Sheet Pan Fajitas

Total Prep Time: 10 Minutes | Total Cook Time: 25 Minutes | Makes: 4 Servings
INGREDIENTS:
- 8 corn tortillas
- 2 tablespoons olive oil
- 1 onion, sliced
- 3 cloves garlic, minced
- 2 bell peppers, sliced thin
- 1 teaspoon salt
- 2 limes, divided
- 1 tablespoon chili powder
- 1/2 cup Greek yogurt
- 3/4 teaspoon paprika
- 1 teaspoon cayenne
- 2 boneless, skinless chicken breasts, sliced thin
- 1/2 tablespoon cumin

DIRECTIONS:
1. Drizzle olive oil over chicken, onions, peppers, and garlic on a rimmed baking sheet.
2. Whisk chili powder, cumin, cornstarch, paprika, salt, and cayenne pepper and season chicken and the vegetables.
3. Bake the chicken and vegetables for 25 minutes at 425 degrees.
4. Meanwhile, zest and juice a lime, then combine with Greek yogurt.
5. Serve the fajitas with a side of Greek yogurt and lime wedges.

NUTRITION

280 Calories, 7g Fat (1g Saturated), 236mg Sodium, 34g Carbohydrates (6g fiber, 5g Sugar), 23g Protein

72. <u>Mediterranean Chicken and quinoa soup</u>

Total Prep Time: 10 Minutes | Total Cook Time: 20 Minutes | Makes: 6 Servings

INGREDIENTS:

- 1 onion, chopped
- 4 cups fat-free, low-sodium chicken broth
- 1 tablespoon thyme, chopped
- 1 cup water
- 3 large garlic cloves, minced
- 1 carrot, sliced
- 1 teaspoon pepper
- 1 lb. boneless, skinless chicken breasts, cubed
- 1/2 cup uncooked quinoa
- 1 dried bay leaf
- 2 ounces sugar snap peas, sliced

DIRECTIONS

1. Bring the chicken, broth, onion, water, carrot, garlic, thyme, bay leaf, and pepper to a boil.
2. Cover and simmer for 5 minutes.
3. Stir in the quinoa thoroughly.
4. Bake for 5 minutes at 350°F.
5. Stir in the peas thoroughly for 8 minutes.
6. Remove the bay leaf and serve.

NUTRITION

Calories: 154, Total Fat: 2.5 g (Saturated Fat: .5 g, Unsaturated Fat: 1 g), Cholesterol: 48 Mg Sodium: 139 Mg, Total Carbohydrate: 12 g (Dietary Fiber: 2 g, Sugar: 3 g), Protein: 20 g

73. <u>Chicken Cauliflower Casserole</u>

Total Prep Time: 15 Minutes | Total Cook Time: 1 Hour 15 Minutes | Makes: 10 Servings

INGREDIENTS:

- 2 tablespoons coconut oil
- 2-2½ pounds bone-in chicken thighs and drumsticks
- Salt and ground black pepper
- 2 garlic cloves, crushed
- 1 teaspoon ground cinnamon
- ½ teaspoon ground turmeric
- 3 carrots, peeled and sliced
- 1 teaspoon paprika
- 2 teaspoons cumin powder
- ¼ teaspoon cayenne pepper
- 28-ounce can of tomatoes with liquid
- 2 tablespoons ginger, chopped
- 1 teaspoon of salt
- 1 head cauliflower, shredded
- 1 onion, chopped
- 1 teaspoon coriander powder
- 1 bell pepper, sliced
- 1 lemon, thinly sliced
- Fresh parsley, crumbled

DIRECTIONS:

1. Preheat your oven to 375°F.
2. Melt 1 tablespoon coconut oil and brown chicken for 5 minutes per side. Set aside.
3. Sauté the carrot, onion, garlic, and ginger for about 4 minutes.
4. Add the spices and remaining coconut oil and stir.
5. Add the chicken, tomatoes, peppers, parsley, and salt and simmer for about 3-5 minutes.
6. Layer the cauliflower rice on the bottom of a rectangular baking dish.
7. Spoon chicken mixture evenly over cauliflower rice and garnish with lemon wedges.
8. Bake for 1 hour.

NUTRITION

Calories: 265| Fat: 16.8g | Carbs: 11.4g | Fiber: 4.2g | Sugars: 4.9g | Protein: 20

74. Salmon Fettuccini

Total Prep Time: 15 Minutes| Total Cook Time: 15 Minutes | Makes: 6 Servings

INGREDIENTS
- 12 ounces fresh salmon, cut into fillets
- Fresh basil
- Sea salt and pepper to taste
- 1 tablespoon clarified butter
- Juice one lemon, about 3 tablespoons
- 2 cloves garlic, minced
- 12 ounces spelt fettuccini, cooked
- 20 spinach leaves

DIRECTIONS
1. Preheat the grill.
2. Gently rub salmon with salt & pepper, then grill for 6 minutes per side until the it readily flakes with a fork.
3. Heat lemon juice, and garlic with butter.
4. Toss pasta, garlic-butter sauce, spinach, and fresh basil in a serving dish.

NUTRITION
Calories 524| Fat 12g (Saturated 3g) | Cholesterol 62mg| Sodium 233mg| Carbohydrate 76g| Dietary Fiber 10g| Protein 35g.

75. Orange Poached Salmon

Total Prep Time: 15 Minutes| Total Cook Time: 15 Minutes | Makes: 3 Servings

INGREDIENTS:
- 1 teaspoon ginger, minced
- 1/2 cup fresh orange juice
- 3 tablespoons coconut aminos
- 4 garlic cloves, crushed
- 3 salmon fillets

DIRECTIONS:
1. Mix all the ingredients except the salmon.
2. Layer salmon fillets in a skillet and spread the ginger mixture over the salmon; bring to a boil.
3. Simmer, covered, for 9 minutes.

NUTRITION
Calories: 259| Fat: 10.6g | Carbs: 7.3g | Fiber: 0.2g| Sugars: 2.4g | Protein: 33.4g

76. <u>Paprika salmon</u>

Total Prep Time: 10 Minutes| Total Cook Time: 8 Minutes | Makes: 6 Servings

INGREDIENTS:
- ½ tablespoon ground ginger
- ½ tablespoon ground coriander
- ½ tablespoon ground cumin
- ½ teaspoon paprika
- ¼ teaspoon cayenne pepper
- Pinch of salt
- 1 tablespoon of fresh orange juice
- 1 tablespoon coconut oil, melted
- 6 salmon fillets

DIRECTIONS:
1. Preheat the gas grill and coat the grill grate with oil.
2. Place all ingredients except salmon in a bowl and stir until paste forms.
3. Add the salmon and brush generously with the mixture.
4. Allow 30 minutes in the refrigerator to marinate.
5. Grill salmon for about 4 minutes on each side.

NUTRITION
Calories: 175| Fat: 9.5g| Carbohydrates: 1 g| Fiber: 0.2g| Sugars: 0.3 g| Protein: 22.2g

77. Honey & Amino Glazed salmon

Total Prep Time: 15 Minutes | Total Cook Time: 15 Minutes | Makes: 6 Servings

INGREDIENTS:
- 1 shallot, chopped
- 1 teaspoon garlic powder
- ¼ cup raw honey
- 1/3 cup fresh orange juice
- 1/3 cup coconut aminos
- 6 salmon fillets
- 1 teaspoon ginger powder

DIRECTIONS:
1. Put all the ingredients in a Ziploc bag and seal the bag.
2. Shake the bag to coat the salmon mixture.
3. Preheat grill to medium heat.
4. Remove the salmon from the marinade bag and set it aside.
5. Grill for about 15 minutes.

NUTRITION
Calories: 216| Fat: 7.1g | Carbs: 16.5g | Fiber: 0.2g| Sugars: 12.9g | Protein: 22.3g

78. Almond Balsamic Beans

Total Prep Time: 10 Minutes | Total Cook Time: 15 Minutes | Makes: 4 Servings

INGREDIENTS:
- 2 tablespoons ground almonds
- 1 pound green beans
- 1 tablespoon olive oil
- 1½ tablespoons balsamic vinegar

DIRECTIONS:

1. Steam the green beans with olive oil and balsamic vinegar.
2. Add the almonds just before serving.

NUTRITION

Calories: 316 | Fat: 27g | Saturated Fat: 3g | Carbohydrates: 15g | Fiber: 6g | Protein: 8g

79. <u>Turmeric Roasted Cauliflower</u>

Total Prep Time: 20 Minutes | Total Cook Time: 10 Minutes | Makes: 5 Servings

INGREDIENTS:

- 8 cups cauliflower florets
- 3 tablespoons olive oil (extra-virgin)
- ½ teaspoon cumin powder
- ½ teaspoon of salt
- 2 teaspoons turmeric powder
- 2 teaspoons lemon juice
- ½ teaspoon black pepper
- 2 large garlic cloves, crushed

DIRECTIONS:

1. Preheat the oven to 425 degrees Fahrenheit.
2. Whisk together oil, turmeric, cumin, salt, pepper, and garlic in a bowl.
3. Add cauliflower and move to a rimmed baking sheet.
4. Roast until golden brown and tender.
5. Drizzle the lemon juice on top.

NUTRITION

124 calories | Protein 3.5g | carbohydrates 9.6 g | dietary fiber 3.7g | sugar 3.3g | fat 8.9g | saturated fat 1.4g

80. <u>Crusted Salmon with dill</u>

Total Prep Time: 15 Minutes | Total Cook Time: 20 Minutes | Makes: 4 Servings

INGREDIENTS:

- 1 cup almonds, ground
- Pinch black pepper
- 1 tablespoon fresh dill, chopped
- 4 teaspoons fresh lemon juice
- 2 tablespoons fresh lemon zest, grated
- ½ teaspoons garlic salt
- 1 tablespoon olive oil
- 4 tablespoons Dijon mustard
- 4 salmon fillets

DIRECTIONS:

1. Pulse the dill, lemon zest, garlic salt, black pepper, and butter into a crumbly mixture.
2. Layer salmon on a rimmed baking sheet
3. Spread Dijon mustard on top of each salmon fillet.
4. Spread the nut mixture evenly over each fillet.
5. Bake for about 15 minutes.

NUTRITION

Calories:350| Fat: 27.8g | Carbs: 5.2g | Fiber: 2.9g| Sugars: 0.8 g | Protein: 24.9g

81. <u>Black pepper Peach and salmon</u>

Total Prep Time: 15 Minutes| Total Cook Time: 12 Minutes | Makes: 4 Servings

INGREDIENTS:

- Pinch Salt
- 4 salmon steaks
- 3 peaches, cored and quartered
- 1 tablespoon fresh ginger, chopped
- 1 teaspoon fresh thyme leaves, chopped
- 1 tablespoon balsamic vinegar
- 3 tablespoons of olive oil
- Pinch ground black pepper

DIRECTIONS:

1. Preheat grill to medium heat.
2. Rub salmon gently with salt and black pepper.
3. Grill peaches and salmon for 5 minutes on each side.
4. Combine the remaining ingredients and spoon over the salmon.
5. Serve with the peaches and onions.

NUTRITION

Calories: 290| Fat: 17.9g | Carbs: 11.7g | Fiber: 2g | Sugars: 10.6g | Protein: 23.2g

82. <u>Sea bass with vegetables</u>

Total Prep Time: 15 Minutes| Total Cook Time: 15 Minutes | Makes: 2 Servings

INGREDIENTS:
- 1 sea bass fillet, diced
- 1 tablespoon coconut vinegar
- ¼ teaspoon garlic paste
- ¼ cup yellow bell peppers, seeded and diced
- 1 teaspoon red pepper powder
- 1 tablespoon olive oil, extra-virgin
- ½ cup fresh button mushrooms, sliced
- 1 small onion, quartered
- ¼ teaspoon ginger paste
- ¼ cup red bell pepper, seeded and diced
- Pinch of salt
- 2-3 spring onions, chopped
- 1 teaspoon fish sauce

DIRECTIONS:
1. Combine fish, ginger, garlic, chili powder, and salt in a bowl and let sit for about 20 minutes.
2. Heat 1 teaspoon of oil in a skillet and sear the fish for 4 minutes on all sides. Set aside.
3. Heat the remaining oil and cook the mushrooms and onions, about 6 minutes.
4. Sauté the peppers and salmon for around 2 minutes.
5. Toss in the spring onions and fish sauce and cook for about 3 minutes.

NUTRITION
Calories: 280| Fat: 17.6g | Carbs: 8.8g | Fiber: 2.2g| Sugars: 3.8g | Protein: 23.9g

83. <u>Pinto & Red Bean Chili</u>

Total Prep Time: 10 Minutes| Total Cook Time: 55 Minutes | Makes: 4 Servings

INGREDIENTS
- 28-ounce can of crushed tomatoes
- 1 yellow onion, chopped
- 3 garlic cloves, minced
- 1 cup water
- 1 tablespoon olive oil
- ½ teaspoon dried marjoram

- ¼ teaspoon ground cayenne
- Salt and freshly ground black pepper
- 2 tablespoons chili powder
- 1½ cups cooked pinto beans
- 2 serrano chiles, seeded and minced
- 3 cups cooked dark red kidney beans

DIRECTIONS
1. Heat the oil and sauté the onion, chiles, and garlic, about 10 minutes.
2. Toss in the tomatoes, water, chili powder, marjoram, cayenne, and season with salt and pepper. Bring to a boil, then reduce to low heat, add the pinto and kidney beans, and cook, covered, for 30 minutes, stirring regularly.
3. Taste and adjust seasonings as needed before continuing to cook, uncovered, for another 15 minutes. Serve right away.

NUTRITION
Calories:350 | Fat: 27.8g | Carbs: 5.2g | Fiber: 2.9g | Sugars: 0.8 g | Protein: 24.9g

84. <u>Red Bean Stew from Jamaica</u>

Total Prep Time: 10 Minutes | Total Cook Time: 40 Minutes | Makes: 4 Servings

INGREDIENTS
- 1 yellow onion, chopped
- 2 carrots, cut into slices
- ½ cup water
- 13.5-ounce can of coconut milk
- 2 garlic cloves, minced
- ¼ teaspoon black pepper
- 1 sweet potato, peeled and diced
- 3 cups cooked dark red kidney beans, drained and rinsed
- 1 tablespoon olive oil
- 1 teaspoon hot or mild curry powder
- 1 teaspoon dried thyme
- ¼ teaspoon ground allspice
- ½ teaspoon salt
- 14.5-ounce can of diced tomatoes, drained

DIRECTIONS
1. Heat the oil in a saucepan and cook the onion and carrots, about 4 minutes.
2. Add garlic, sweet potato, and red pepper followed by kidney beans, tomatoes, curry powder, thyme, allspice, salt, and black pepper.
3. Stir in the water, and simmer, covered, for 30 minutes.
4. Stir in the coconut milk right at the end..

NUTRITION
Calories 160 | Fat 3g (Saturated 0g) | Cholesterol 0mg | Sodium 549mg | Carbohydrate 30g | Dietary Fiber 5g | Protein 8g.

85. <u>Aubergine Mediterranean Chilli</u>

Total Prep Time: 10 Minutes| Total Cook Time: 10 Minutes | Makes: 4 Servings

INGREDIENTS:
- 1 red onion, finely chopped
- Coconut or olive oil
- 1 aubergine cut into cubes
- 2 garlic cloves, crushed
- 5 small red chilies, chopped
- 1/2 teaspoons coriander powder
- 1 teaspoon of cumin powder
- 1 teaspoon of cinnamon powder
- 1 can of tomatoes
- 2 cups black beans, cooked
- Sea salt
- Freshly ground black pepper
- 2 serves of brown rice, quinoa, or couscous

DIRECTIONS:
1. Melt the coconut oil and fry the aubergines for 4 minutes. Set aside.
2. Sauté the onions and garlic, then add the chiles for 4 minutes.
3. Add the tomatoes, coriander, seasonings, and aubergine, and cook for 5 minutes.
4. Add the black beans and cook for 9 minutes.

NUTRITION
Calories 160| Fat 3g (Saturated 0g) | Cholesterol 0mg| Sodium 549mg| Carbohydrate 30g| Dietary Fiber 5g| Protein 8g.

86. <u>Fall Pumpkin Soup</u>

Total Prep Time: 25 Minutes| Total Cook Time: 40 Minutes | Makes: 6 Servings

INGREDIENTS:
- 600 g pumpkin, peeled and chopped
- 2 cups of vegetable broth
- 1 teaspoon of cumin powder
- ½ cup coconut milk
- frying oil
- 1 tablespoon lemongrass, chopped
- 1 ginger, peeled and grated
- 2 kaffir lime leaves, chopped
- 1 teaspoon coriander seeds
- 1 red pepper, seeded and sliced

- 1 fresh turmeric, peeled and sliced
- Black pepper to taste
- 1 shallot, chopped
- 4 garlic cloves

DIRECTIONS:
1. Toss the squash in the oil before placing it on the baking sheet and roasting until golden brown.
2. In a pan, heat the oil and sauté the shallots until brown.
3. Add cumin and coriander.
4. Add the kaffir leaves, turmeric, ginger, lemongrass, and chili, and cook for another minute, stirring to avoid burning
5. Add the squash to the broth then cover and cook
6. Simmer for another 10 minutes.
7. Add the coconut milk and cook for 6 minutes.

NUTRITION
Calories: 192 | Fat: 15g

87. Barley vegetable soup

Total Prep Time: 5 Minutes | Total Cook Time: 40 Minutes | Makes: 6 Servings

INGREDIENTS:
- 1 cup carrots, chopped
- 1 clove of garlic, minced
- 3/4 cup peeled barley
- Vegan parmesan, Grated
- 4 cups vegetable broth
- 1 cup celery, chopped
- 28-ounce can of tomato purée
- 15-ounce can of beans, drained and rinsed
- 2 cups kale, coarsely chopped
- 1 sprig of rosemary

DIRECTIONS:
1. Cook the onions, carrots, and celery with olive oil in a pan.
2. Add the rosemary, garlic, and barley.
3. Bring the broth to a boil, constantly stirring.
4. Reduce the heat to low, and cook for about 1 hour until the barley is cooked, then add the tomatoes and beans.
5. Serve with vegan parmesan.

NUTRITION
Calories: 277.37 | Carbs: 52.82g | Protein: 7.43g | Fats: 5.9g | Fiber: 9.1g

88. <u>Squash and Lentil Soup</u>

Total Prep Time: 10 Minutes | Total Cook Time: 40 Minutes | Makes: 4-6 Servings

INGREDIENTS:
- 8 cups of vegetable broth
- 1 large onion, diced
- 1 peeled and diced butternut squash
- 1 cup brown lentils
- 2 teaspoons minced garlic
- 1 bay leaf
- 1/2 teaspoon ground nutmeg
- 1 cup spinach, chopped
- 1/2 teaspoon of salt

DIRECTIONS:
1. Add all ingredients except spinach to your slow cooker and mix well.
2. Simmer for 8 hours.
3. Remove the bay leaf.
4. Add chopped spinach and stir until softened.

NUTRITION
Calories: 167 | Fat: 5g | Saturated: 1g | Carbohydrate: 23g | Fiber: 3g | Protein: 6g

89. <u>Rosemary Pasta Shells Soup</u>

Total Prep Time: 8 Minutes | Total Cook Time: 25 Minutes | Makes: 4 Servings

INGREDIENTS
- 2 teaspoons olive oil
- Pinch red pepper flakes
- 1/2 cup whole wheat pasta shells
- 1 shallot, finely diced
- 1 garlic clove, minced
- 14.5-ounce can of white beans
- 3 Cups Baby Spinach, cleaned and trimmed
- 1/8 teaspoon black pepper
- 4 cups fat-free chicken broth
- 1 teaspoon rosemary
- 14.5-ounce can of diced tomatoes

DIRECTIONS

1. Preheat the oven to 350°F.
2. Heat the oil and cook garlic and shallot for 4 minutes.
3. Add the broth, tomatoes, beans, rosemary, and black and red pepper to taste.
4. Cook until they begin to boil.
5. Add the noodles.
6. Finally, stir in the spinach.

NUTRITION
Calories 218.4, Fat 3.3 g, Carbohydrates 37.9 g, Protein 12 g

90. <u>Bell pasta with kidney beans</u>

Total Prep Time: 10 Minutes| Total Cook Time: 40 Minutes | Makes: 8 Servings
INGREDIENTS
- 3 Cups low fat, low chicken broth
- 1 cup whole tomatoes, chopped
- 1 cup seashell pasta
- 2 cups kidney beans, cooked
- 1 onion, chopped
- 2 teaspoon chopped fresh thyme
- 1/2 cup chopped spinach
- 1 red bell pepper, chopped
- 1 tablespoon olive oil
- 2 cloves garlic, minced
- Pinch ground black pepper to taste

DIRECTIONS
1. Preheat a pot.
2. Heat oil and cook onion, bell pepper, and garlic for 3 minutes.
3. Mix in the broth, tomatoes, and beans and simmer for 20 minutes.
4. Mix in the thyme, spinach, and pasta and cook another 5 minutes.
5. Season with salt and pepper.

NUTRITION
Calories 174 kcal, Fat 3.1 g, Carbohydrates 29g, Protein 8 g

91. <u>Rigatoni Pasta Casserole</u>

Total Prep Time: 30 Minutes| Total Cook Time: 55 Minutes | Makes: 6 Servings

INGREDIENTS

- 16-ounce rigatoni pasta, cooked
- 1/2 teaspoon garlic, minced
- 1 lb. ground sausage
- 1/4 cup Romano cheese, grated
- 28-ounce can of Italian-style tomato sauce
- Parsley, to garnish
- 3 cups shredded mozzarella cheese
- 14-ounce can cannellini beans, drained and rinsed
- 1 teaspoon Italian seasoning

DIRECTIONS

1. Preheat the oven to 350 degrees Fahrenheit.
2. Using butter or oil, grease a casserole dish.
3. Cook garlic and sausages for 6 minutes and then add tomato sauce, beans, and Italian seasoning; simmer for 5 minutes.
4. Half of the sausage pasta mixture should be poured into the oiled casserole, followed by half of the mozzarella cheese. To make another layer, repeat the process.
5. Place a piece of foil on top of the dish and top it with Romano cheese.
6. Bake the rigatoni casserole for 26 minutes.

NUTRITION

Calories 795.6, Fat 37.6 g, Cholesterol 166.2 mg, Sodium 1842.2 mg, Carbohydrates 73.2, Protein 41.2 g

92. <u>Vegetable Mediterranean Pasta</u>

Total Prep Time: 10 Minutes| Total Cook Time: 10 Minutes | Makes: 4 Servings

INGREDIENTS:

- 1/2 pack of vegetable or spelt pasta, cooked
- 1 courgette
- 1 medium broccoli
- 5 garlic gloves
- Chilies, diced
- 4 tomatoes
- A handful of basil leaves
- 1 tablespoon of olive oil
- Himalayan salt and black pepper.

DIRECTIONS:

1. Heat the oil on a low, gentle heat, and sauté the garlic, basil, and chili for two minutes.
2. Add the remaining vegetables, which have been sliced to make them tiny and easy to cook.
3. Cook everything for another two minutes.

NUTRITION
Calories 160| Fat 3g (Saturated 0g) | Cholesterol 0mg| Sodium 549mg| Carbohydrate 30g| Dietary Fiber 5g| Protein 8g.

93. <u>Tomato & Cauliflower Spaghetti</u>

Total Prep Time: 5 Minutes| Total Cook Time: 5 Minutes | Makes: 4 Servings
INGREDIENTS:
- 1 tablespoon olive oil
- 125g sun-blushed tomatoes, chopped
- 1 shallot, finely chopped
- 1 garlic clove, finely chopped
- Handful of rocket
- Handful of spinach
- Handful of cauliflower, chopped
- Handful chive, chopped
- ½ lemon, juice only
- 250g spelt spaghetti, cooked

DIRECTIONS:
1. Heat the coconut oil and sauté the shallot, garlic, and tomatoes very gently.
2. Add the lemon juice.
3. Serve on top of the spaghetti.

NUTRITION
157 calories| Protein 7.8g| carbohydrates 24.2g | dietary fiber 3.7g | sugar 3.1 g | fat 8.3g | saturated fat 4.3g

94. <u>No-bake pumpkin cheesecake</u>

Total Prep Time: 20 Minutes + Freezing Time | Makes: 2 Servings

INGREDIENTS
FOR THE CRUST
- 3/4 cup Almond Flour
- 1/2 cup Flaxseed Meal
- 1/4 cup butter

FOR THE FILLING
- 6 oz. Cream Cheese
- 1/3 cup Pumpkin Purée
- 2 tablespoons Sour Cream
- 1/4 cup Heavy Cream

- 1 teaspoon Pumpkin Pie Spice
- 25 drops of Liquid Stevia

- 3 tablespoons Butter
- 1/4 teaspoon Pumpkin Pie Spice
- 25 drops of Liquid Stevia

DIRECTIONS
1. Mix all of the crust's dry ingredients thoroughly.
2. Mash together the dry ingredients with the butter and liquid stevia until a dough forms.
3. Place the dough in your mini tart pans.
4. Blitz all filling ingredients using a blender and refrigerate.
5. After about 5 hours, Slice, and top with whipped cream.

NUTRITION
266 Calories, 23g Fats, 3g Carbohydrates, 4g Protein.

95. <u>Crusty Peanut butter bars</u>

Total Prep Time: 10 Minutes| Total Cook Time: 15 Minutes | Makes: 2 Servings

INGREDIENTS
CRUST
- 1/2 teaspoon Cinnamon
- Pinch of Salt
- 1 cup Almond Flour

FUDGE
- 1/4 cup Erythritol
- 1/4 cup Heavy Cream
- 1/8 teaspoon Xanthan Gum

TOPPING
- 1/3 cup Chocolate, Chopped

- 1 tablespoon Erythritol
- 1/4 cup butter, melted

- 1/4 cup butter, melted
- 1/2 cup Peanut Butter
- 1/2 teaspoon Vanilla Extract

DIRECTIONS
1. Preheat the oven to 400 degrees Fahrenheit.
2. Mix almond flour with half of the melted butter followed by erythritol and cinnamon.
3. Press into a lined baking dish and bake for 10 minutes.
4. Blend all of the fudge ingredients and spread up the sides of the baking dish.
5. Top your bars with chopped chocolate just before cooling.
6. Remove the bars by peeling the parchment paper out once they have cooled.

NUTRITION
Calories 795.6, Fat 37.6 g, Cholesterol 166.2 mg, Sodium 1842.2 mg, Carbohydrates 73.2, Protein 41.2 g

96. Pumpkin and Date ice cream

Total Prep Time: 15 Minutes + Freezing Time| Makes: 6 Servings

INGREDIENTS:
- ½ teaspoon vanilla extract
- 15 ounces pumpkin purée
- 2 cans of unsweetened coconut milk
- ½ cup dates, pitted and chopped
- ½ teaspoon ground cinnamon
- 1½ teaspoons pumpkin pie spice

DIRECTIONS:
1. Blend all the ingredients until smooth.
2. Freeze for up to 2 hours.

3. Pour the mixture into an ice cream machine halfway and process.
4. Freeze the ice cream for around 1 to 2 hours before serving it in an airtight container.

NUTRITION
Calories: 293| Fat: 22.5g | Carbs: 24.8g | Fiber: 3.6g| Sugars: 14.1g | Protein: 2.3g

97. <u>Mediterranean pumpkin cream</u>

Total Prep Time: 15 Minutes | Total Cook Time: 1 Hour | Makes: 6 Servings

INGREDIENTS:
- 9 drops of liquid stevia
- 1 cup canned pumpkin
- 1 teaspoon cinnamon powder
- 1 teaspoon vanilla extract
- ¼ teaspoon ginger powder
- pinch of salt
- 2 teaspoons of nutmeg powder
- 2 eggs, beaten
- 1 cup coconut milk

DIRECTIONS:
1. Preheat your oven to 350°F.
2. Mix the pumpkin and spices.
3. Mix eggs with other ingredients.
4. Add egg mixture to pumpkin mixture and stir until well blended.
5. Transfer the mixture to 6 ramekins.
6. Pour water around the ramekins.
7. Bake for at least 1 hour.

NUTRITION
Calories: 130| Fat: 11.1g | Carbs: 6.1g | Fiber: 2.3g| Sugars: 2.9g | Protein: 3.3g

98. <u>Very spicy Pumpkin pie</u>

Total Prep Time: 15 Minutes | Total Cook Time: 1 Hour 15 Minutes | Makes: 8 Servings

INGREDIENTS:
FOR THE CRUST:
- 1 teaspoon baking powder
- 2 tablespoons coconut oil
- 2½ cups almonds
- 1 teaspoon of sal

FOR FILLING:
- 1 can (15 ounces) of unsweetened pumpkin purée
- 1 tablespoon arrowroot powder
- ½ teaspoon nutmeg powder
- ½ teaspoon cinnamon powder
- ¼ teaspoon ginger powder
- 3 tablespoons raw honey
- ¼ teaspoon cardamom powder
- ¼ teaspoon ground cloves
- pinch of salt
- 1 cup coconut milk
- 3 eggs, beaten

DIRECTIONS:
1. Preheat your oven to 350°F.
2. For the crust, add the nuts, baking soda, coconut oil, and salt to a processor and pulse.
3. Place crust mixture in a 9-inch cake pan.
4. Bake for about 15 minutes.
5. Combine all the filling ingredients.
6. Remove the crust from the oven.
7. Spoon the mixture into the crust.
8. Bake for about 50 minutes.
9. Freeze about 3-4 hours before serving.

NUTRITION
Calories: 411 | Fat: 35.5g | Carbs: 17.8g | Fiber: 5g | Sugars: 9.8g | Protein: 12.8g

99. Mediterranean Pumpkin cake

Total Prep Time: 10 Minutes| Total Cook Time: 20 Minutes | Makes: 4 Servings

INGREDIENTS:
- 1 cup pumpkin purée
- 2 cups blanched almond flour
- 2 teaspoons ground cinnamon
- a few drops of stevia
- ½ cup flaxseed meal
- 1 tablespoon vanilla extract
- ½ teaspoon low sodium salt
- 1 egg

DIRECTIONS:
1. Mix almond flour, flaxseed meal, cinnamon, and salt.
2. Combine the egg, pumpkin, and vanilla extract with the help of a spatula.
3. To make a batter, gently combine the dry and wet components, being careful not to overmix or the batter will become greasy and dense.
4. Spoon into a lined pan and bake at 350°F for 20 minutes.

NUTRITION
Calories: 125 | Fat: 0.5 | Carbohydrates: 25 | Fiber: 1 | Protein: 4.5

100. Raspberry lemon popsicles

Total Prep Time: 2 Hours | Makes: 6 Servings

INGREDIENTS
- 100G Raspberries
- 1/4 cup Heavy Cream
- Juice 1/2 Lemon
- 20 drops of Liquid Stevia
- 1/2 teaspoon Guar Gum
- 1/4 cup Coconut Oil
- 1 cup Coconut Milk
- 1/4 cup Sour Cream

DIRECTIONS

1. Blitz all ingredients with an immersion blender.
2. Blend until the raspberries are thoroughly combined with the remaining ingredients.
3. Strain the mixture, ensuring that all raspberry seeds are removed.
4. Fill the molds with the mixture.
5. Freeze the popsicles for at least 2 hours before serving.
6. To remove the popsicles from the mold, run them under hot water.

NUTRITION

156 Calories, 16g Fats, 2g Carbohydrates, 0.5g Protein.

CONCLUSION

This diet is full of Fruits, vegetables, fish, olive oil, whole grains, legumes, and nuts which are all healthful and nutritional and provide overall wellness.

As a result of its high fiber content, the diet is good for the gut and can help keep bowel motions regular and smooth. The diet also contributes to the growth of beneficial gut flora, which aids in a variety of physiological processes, including immunity and overall health.

This diet's anti-oxidant and anti-inflammatory components can also help to slow down the aging process and promote brain function. Consumers, particularly postmenopausal women, benefit from the calcium-rich components of this diet, which improve bone and muscle health. Diabetes, dyslipidemia (high cholesterol), memory loss and dementia, breast cancer, depression, and other disorders are all prevented by eating a healthy diet. According to specialists, it also aids in maintaining a healthy body weight.

And the best thing is that unlike most other diets, the Mediterranean diet is simple to follow and to stick to!

30 DAYS MEAL PLAN

Day	BREAKFAST	LUNCH	DINNER	SNACK/DESSERT
WEEK 1				
1	Pork Cracklins With Eggs	Mixed Green Salad with Beets	Barley vegetable soup	Mediterranean Fried Queso Blanco
2	Italian pizza waffles	Spinach, Shrimp & Tangerine Bowl	Rigatoni Pasta Casserole	Mini Portobello pizzas
3	Nutmeg-Spiced Quinoa porridge	Split Peas with Spinach	Sea bass with vegetables	Mediterranean Pumpkin cake
4	Blueberry Cinnamon Breakfast Bake	Mediterranean Spinach and potatoes	Sheet Pan Fajitas	Ham and Cheese Stromboli
5	Quick Oats with coconut milk	Snow Peas & Spaghetti	Almond Balsamic Beans	Raspberry lemon popsicles
6	Spicy Sweet potato Breakfast Bowl	Roasted Lemon Herb Chicken	Vegetable Mediterranean Pasta	Olive Pizza bombs
7	Cinnamon Chia Pudding	Farro Salad with Sweet Pea Pesto	Black pepper Peach and salmon	Cocoa peanut butter bombs
WEEK 2				
8	Apple Cinnamon Chia	Low Sodium Salad with Capers	Mediterranean Chicken and quinoa soup	Pizza Breadsticks
9	Apple Almond Coconut Bowl	Mango, Jalapeno & bean salad	Seared Chicken & Tomatoes	Tortilla chips
10	Cinnamon quinoa with peach & Pecan	Mixed Green Salad with Beets	Sheet Pan Fajitas	Sweet Potato Chicken Dumplings
11	Pecan Porridge with Banana	Veggie-Stuffed Tomatoes	Pinto & Red Bean Chili	Mediterranean Edamame
12	Apple Almond Coconut Bowl	Mediterranean Ratatouille	Chicken Cauliflower Casserole	Tofu and Capers Pizza
13	Pecan Porridge with Banana	Mediterranean Spinach and potatoes	Paprika salmon	Jalapeno popper bombs
14	Quick Oats with coconut milk	Aubergine, Potato & Chickpea	Crusted Salmon with dill	Tortilla chips
WEEK 3				

15	Spicy Sweet potato Breakfast Bowl	Roman Tuna Salad	Bell pasta with kidney beans	Rotisserie chicken pizza
16	Walnut and almond porridge	Mixed Green Salad with Beets	Orange Poached Salmon	Neapolitan bombs
17	Protein Almond Muesli	Hearty Cauliflower Rice with chicken	Red Bean Stew from Jamaica	Crusty Peanut butter bars
18	Pecan Porridge with Banana	Spicy Turkey Stir Fry	Turmeric Roasted Cauliflower	Corndog Muffins
19	Quick Oats with coconut milk	Tortellini Salad with Spinach	Creamy Baked Chicken	Very spicy Pumpkin pie
20	Apple Cinnamon Chia	Garlic and sesame noodles	Honey & Amino Glazed salmon	Cocoa peanut butter bombs
21	Cinnamon Millet porridge	Black Pepper Salmon with yogurt	Tomato & Cauliflower Spaghetti	Coconut orange creamsicle bombs
WEEK 4				
22	Walnut and almond porridge	Roman Tuna Salad	Mediterranean Chicken and quinoa soup	Raspberry lemon popsicles
23	Pecan Porridge with Banana	Spinach, Shrimp & Tangerine Bowl	Orange Poached Salmon	Mediterranean Pumpkin cake
24	Apple Almond Coconut Bowl	Mediterranean Ratatouille	Crusted Salmon with dill	Cheesy Ramen Pizzas
25	Apple Almond Coconut Bowl	Stir-Fried Vegetables & Rice	Almond Balsamic Beans	Tofu and Capers Pizza
26	Italian pizza waffles	Mixed Green Salad with Beets	Orange Poached Salmon	Jalapeno popper bombs
27	Spicy Sweet potato Breakfast Bowl	Aubergine, Potato & Chickpea	Crusted Salmon with dill	Raspberry lemon popsicles
28	Italian pizza waffles	Mediterranean Ratatouille	Chicken Cauliflower Casserole	Mediterranean Pumpkin cake
WEEK 5				
29	Walnut and almond porridge	Low Sodium Salad with Capers	Almond Balsamic Beans	Cheesy Ramen Pizzas
30	Apple Almond Coconut Bowl	Roman Tuna Salad	Chicken Cauliflower Casserole	Jalapeno popper bombs

THE COMPLETE MEDITERRANEAN DIET FOOD SHOPPING LIST

VEGETABLES

✓ Tomatoes
✓ Peppers
✓ Onions
✓ Eggplant
✓ Cucumbers
✓ Green beans
✓ Okra
✓ Zucchini
✓ Garlic Peas
✓ Potatoes
✓ Mushrooms
✓ Cauliflower
✓ Broccoli
✓ Carrots
✓ Celery leaves
✓ Beets
✓ Spinach
✓ Cabbage
✓ Romaine
✓ Lettuce
✓ Frozen spinach
✓ Frozen Peas
✓ Green beans

FRUIT
✓ Oranges
✓ Tangerines
✓ Lemons
✓ Apples
✓ Pears
✓ Cherries
✓ Watermelon
✓ Peaches
✓ Figs
✓ Apricots

DAIRY
✓ Greek Yogurt

✓ Feta cheese
✓ Fresh Ricotta
✓ Parmesan
✓ Fresh Mozzarella

DMEAT AND POULTRY
✓ Chicken (whole, legs etc.)
✓ Eggs
✓ Veal
✓ Pork

FISH AND SEAFOOD
✓ Cod
✓ Shrimp Octopus
✓ Salmon
✓ Halibut

GRAINS AND BREADS
✓ Whole grain breadsticks
✓ Pita bread
✓ Phyllo
✓ Pasta Rice
✓ Egg pasta Bulgur
✓ Couscous

GREENS
✓ Chicory
✓ Dandelion
✓ Beet Greens
✓ Amaranth

FATS AND NUTS
✓ Extra Virgin Olive Oil
✓ Tahin
✓ Almonds
✓ Walnuts
✓ Pine Nuts
✓ Pistachios
✓ Sesame seeds
✓ Sunflower seeds

BEANS
✓ Lentils
✓ White beans
✓ Chickpeas
✓ Yellow Split Pea

PANTRY
✓ Canned tomatoes
✓ Tomato Paste
✓ Olives
✓ Sundried Tomatoes
✓ Capers
✓ Balsamic/red wine vinegar
✓ Honey
✓ Wine

HERBS AND SPICES
✓ Oregano
✓ Parsley
✓ Dill
✓ Mint
✓ Basil
✓ Cumin
✓ Paprika
✓ Cinnamon
✓ Pepper/sea sa

INDEX